The French Revolution

J. M. ROBERTS

The French Revolution

1978

OXFORD UNIVERSITY PRESS
OXFORD   LONDON   NEW YORK

Oxford University Press, Walton Street, Oxford OX2 6DP

OXFORD   LONDON   GLASGOW

NEW YORK   TORONTO   MELBOURNE   WELLINGTON

IBADAN   NAIROBI   DAR ES SALAAM   CAPE TOWN

KUALA LUMPUR   SINGAPORE   JAKARTA   HONG KONG   TOKYO

DELHI   BOMBAY   CALCUTTA   MADRAS   KARACHI

British Library Cataloguing in Publication Data

Roberts, John Morris
  The French revolution.
    1. France – Politics and government – 1789–1815
    2. France – History – Revolution, 1789–1815
  I. Title
944.04   DC155   78–40193

ISBN 0–19–215822–5
ISBN 0–19–289069–7 Pbk.

Printed in Great Britain by
Richard Clay (The Chaucer Press) Ltd,
Bungay, Suffolk

Contents

Preface

IN one comprehensible sense the French Revolution is no longer a historical subject, for it can no longer be understood and explained as a unified and cohesive whole even by specialists. This is in part because of the sheer proliferation of printed source material (the unprinted material in so 'administered' a country is effectively limitless) and secondary monographs; scholars must now specialize within the events we call 'the' Revolution and even then they will find it hard to keep up with the flood of relevant publications. But disintegration also follows the intellectual impact of detailed research; it has not only thrown a fog of confusing detail over the landscape but has helped to blow apart the old assumptions of continuity and causality which held a historiographical monolith together. (These assumptions have also suffered from the decline of ideologies which sustained them, of course, though not enough.) Why, then, write another book purporting to be about the French Revolution? More pointed still, why another summary book? Even in the English-speaking world, there are surely enough—a new one every two or three years in this country alone for the last three decades—and there are scores of French surveys calling for attention, too.

The answer to these questions need not, I think, rest on any assumptions about the substantial unity of the subject. What matters is the unity it has in the eye of the beholder: it is a matter of fact that the events of the Revolution dominate the modern historical landscape, so that each generation has to look at them again in the light not only of fresh scholarship but of its own preoccupations.

This still left me (when the editor of this series was kind enough to invite me to contribute to it) wondering what sort of book to write. In the old *Home University Library* (which OPUS books replace) there was a volume on the Revolution by Hilaire Belloc which, clearly, there was no chance at all of refurbishing so as to make it satisfactory for modern readers. 'Up-to-date' narrative (based, that is to say, on recent research) posed almost as many problems of a different kind. In the end, it seemed to me that there might still be a place for a book which did not try to narrate a story in detail—a task in any case impossible in the space available—or even in outline, except where the narrative was needed in order to explain, a book which sought instead to sketch the contours of revolutionary history as it now appears, adding only such specific information as is essential to make its standpoint clear. I have emphasized the way the Revolutionary years brought breaks with the French past, the way they expressed continuities running across them and linking that past to the nineteenth century, and the impact they had outside France, and the legacy they left in the minds of men. In 60,000 words there was not room for much else, I am afraid, though I have added a chronological table of events to provide bearings for readers approaching the Revolution for the first time.

The result is very much a description of one man's view from England, even perhaps from Oxford, in 1977. It will serve its purpose, though, if readers find in it a point of departure. A special orientation can have its own logic and validity, and can be helpful before the plunge is made into more comprehensive and specialized writings.

In this country at least (and possibly in the United States, though I am not sure of that) the knowledge of all foreign languages seems much less widespread among those who read books than fifty years ago. It seems only sensible to recognize this in discussing the Revolution. Though it would be silly to avoid using any French words at all in this book—some technical terms must be understood in order to read other books, even if they are in English—I have translated such passages as are quoted in it, and have always attempted a translation or paraphrase of a technical word or phrase when it first appears. The index will show where this is. I have also limited my suggestions for further reading to books in English, a decision which is by no means a grave handicap at the introductory level of this book; British and American scholars have, happily, made such substantial contributions to Revolutionary history in the last few decades that useful advice can now be given on this basis. Still, anyone who wants to approach the fundamental literature must read French; for this reason, anyone I am fortunate enough to interest in the French Revolution through this book, should take as the immediate next step the learning of French, if only for reading purposes.

The index also includes full names and dates of birth and death of all persons mentioned in the text, but these may be fewer than expected, for I have cut down the number of persons mentioned as much as I dared.

I owe special thanks for the help of three friends and colleagues. Dr. G. J. Ellis was kind enough to read the proofs and the benefit has been immense. At an earlier stage, Dr. Colin Lucas gave me priceless advice, rooting out such errors as the heavy demands of his other work allowed him to seize and tempering my idiosyncrasies with comments on the first draft he read. I am deeply grateful to both these gentlemen, and if the outcome does not satisfy them, that does not mean I did not learn a lot from what they said. To the Editor of the series I also owe my gratitude, both for the indulgence and encouragement he offered me so freely while I was writing, and for his comments on the text.

Merton College, Oxford   J.M.R.

I

Beginnings

THE historian cannot do without the word 'revolution', shapeless and slippery smooth though it is after much use and abuse. It is traditionally applied to some great events and in those instances at least, it is ineradicable. Yet it is very hard to pin down its meaning precisely, even in referring to what happened in France in 1789, surely its most famous use. Much of our modern sense of the word only goes back that far, so that it is not a long history but a rapid expansion of meaning since then that has created the problem.

The roots of the word's modern popularity can be traced back further, but until the later seventeenth century its sense was clearly metaphorical. It reflected the age's awareness of the cyclical movements of the heavens; it was politically almost colourless and in such phrases as 'the revolutions of history' or 'of time' meant little more than 'events' or 'happenings'. The idea of such a revolution could have occasional political application, to changes of ministers, or favourites, for instance, but the word was not for a long time connected indissolubly with political upheaval (it was not, for example, applied to the 'Frondes', the disturbances which paralysed the French monarchy in the middle of the seventeenth century). Then, somewhere towards the year 1700, Frenchmen began to use the word in an especially political way as a result of thinking about what the English called 'the Glorious Revolution' of 1688. Our ancestors had been far from anxious to stress a break with the past; they tried to dress up what had happened as a conservative process which maintained legal continuities, thus preserving something of the old sense of the word, but the French (perhaps because they could sympathize more easily with James II) saw that it was a rupture in more than the personal succession of English kingship.

In the eighteenth century, some people went on using it in its old, pre-political senses, but the new style caught on and the sense of a return or recurrence to a former point gradually ebbed away. To most of us, the idea of an irredeemable break is still the only firm ground in a confused morass of ideas: whatever else it may mean, in writing about the French Revolution, the word denotes a real, if vaguely defined, discontinuity.

Even those who have wanted to argue that the continuities of the 1790s have been underrated have implicitly accepted this much, sometimes by going to the extreme of suggesting that the word should not be used at all for what happened in France at the end of the eighteenth century because there was then no break with the past in any respect that mattered. The essence of 'revolution' in ordinary usage was always contrast with what went before even when the extent of that contrast was misjudged. When an English visitor remarked towards the end of June 1789 that the whole business 'now seems over, and the revolution complete', he was not in fact being silly; he was rightly observing that when absolute monarchy had given way to a demand that a representative body of its subjects should have something like the legislative powers of an English parliament, then a real constitutional change had indeed occurred. It was one he thought important enough to call 'revolution', and his choice of word seems reasonable even if changes just as dramatic were still to follow.

Constitutional discontinuity was for a long time what first caught the eye in the Revolution; it still provides the major landmarks on Frenchmen's mental map of the 1790s. The simplest and most obviously incontrovertible account of 'what happened' in the French Revolution runs somewhat as follows: The old French monarchy was replaced in the summer of 1789 by a new, limited, monarchy in which power was meant to be shared between the King and the representatives of the French people sitting in a National Assembly; when this failed to work, monarchy was set aside in 1792 and the first French republic appeared; in 1793 and 1794 a period of exceptional and centralized government provided a temporary answer to a grave national emergency and little attention was paid to the rights of individuals which had been cherished in 1789 (sometimes this is called the era of 'Revolutionary Government', sometimes simply the 'Terror'); this, in turn, was followed by a relaxation which restored power to the parliamentary body, at that time called the 'Convention'; its members gave France yet another constitution and government by a 'Directory' in 1795 which lasted until a *coup d'état* in 1799 brought the parliamentary system to an end; the final outcome was the installation in power of a 'Consulate', whose outstanding figure was a young general, Bonaparte, and this can reasonably be taken as the last important change defining the elementary chronology of the great crisis in French history called the 'Revolution'.

Such an emphasis on politics and the constitution has long been criticized by some historians for telling us very little; it is a mere history of events (*histoire événementielle*) they say, revealing little about causes. This criticism sometimes seems exaggerated; it would be necessary to go back a very long way to find any serious historian saying that the story of the Revolution could be adequately dealt with *only* in terms of politics. Yet it is true that even for limited purposes such a bald account of one class of discontinuities takes us only a little way. On closer inspection, it appears that even such great upheavals are far from the whole story of the discontinuities in French history brought about by the Revolution. It is worthwhile retracing the same ground from a different point of view—and, indeed, somewhat more ground, for it is now generally agreed that to understand even the events of 1789 it is best to go back at least a little further.

'Pre-Revolution'

Some historians see 1787 as the start of something they call the 'pre-Revolution', a prolonged crisis detonated by a long-postponed attempt to solve old problems. At the heart of them lay the State's penury, expressed most obviously in deficits and a huge debt accumulated, for the most part, in pursuit of an expensive foreign policy. Whether France could remain a great power was not clear in 1787, given the debts which weakened her credit as a borrower and imposed crippling demands on such fiscal resources as lay to hand. These resources, it appeared to many Frenchmen, had to be increased. Their efforts to find ways of doing this explain much of the pre-Revolution.

This was because of the nature of French institutions. Debt was by no means the whole story even in so far as finance was concerned. The structure of the financial machinery itself also militated against efficiency, for much of it was manned by officials and contractors who saw public finance as a mass of private interests. Outside the realm of finance, administrative incoherences multiplied. Rather than the French State, it would be more precise to speak of the French monarchy, for that provided the only formal and legal tie between all those who lived in the lands ruled by Louis XVI. In 1789, the modern State which we take for granted, exercising a probably unlimited legislative sovereignty over everybody living in a fairly coherent block of territory, existed barely anywhere in continental Europe. The realms of the King of France certainly did not look like one; they were a collection of domains and provinces where his legal powers (and those of his officers) varied from place to place. In some, local representative bodies were eager in defence of prescriptive rights they feared might be infringed; elsewhere, local privileges inherited from formal contracts embodied old judicial and legal immunities. No common law ran everywhere in France, nor, so far as political institutions went, was there any French nation.

This helps to explain a distinction dear to French lawyers when they discussed their constitution. An Englishman might feel that a country without the writ *habeas corpus*, where people could be detained indefinitely at the royal pleasure (that is to say, at the pleasure of advisers who could persuade the royal council to authorize such a detention), was a despotism. French constitutionalists rebutted the charge. The French Crown was not despotic, they said, but 'absolute'. No authority existed which would override the royal will, but it could not be legally exercised except within limits. Often during the eighteenth century, lawyers had taken it upon themselves to assert that specific acts of royal authority were unlawful. They never alleged that the King was to blame, but only that he had been badly advised by unscrupulous counsellors; his will had been 'surprised', was their conventional way of putting it. Such lawyers had usually made their views known collectively, through the corporations to which they belonged, the 'sovereign courts', which provided not only the main judicial structure of France, but also institutions protecting their professional interests and, sometimes and in moderate measure, acted as outlets for local and popular grievance. Of these courts the most important were the thirteen *parlements*; among them the *Parlement* of Paris was pre-eminent.

The monarchy, deploying its executive impetus through royal councils, ministers, and a network of officials, represented the centralizing principle and provided the institutions which brought eighteenth-century France closest to being a modern State. But the French constitution could also be viewed as the incoherent mass of rights and privileges which belonged to individuals and to corporations. Among the corporations were bodies with widely differing natures and powers. The *parlements* have been mentioned, but guilds of master-workmen were corporations, too; so were some provinces, the ruling bodies of some towns, and religious orders and monastic houses. The French Church was the greatest corporation of all. A man might be a member of more than one such corporation and his own legal standing depended on the rights—privileges was the usual eighteenth-century word—this gave him. Not only private but public life was rooted in this setting. Public policy was discussed in terms of its effects upon the legal rights of interested parties; no one willingly accepted that such rights could be overridden and no one thought they could be legislated away, for no power to utter such legislation existed. This was another reason why lawyers were so important and their arguments so persuasive. Even the mode in which laws were made suggested this, for royal edicts were not enforceable in the courts until they had been 'registered' as a part of the law those courts would administer. Implicit in this was the idea that truly innovatory laws were never made (and, indeed, *could* not be made); all that was happening was that the principles of existing law were being invoked in a new way.

One way of summarizing this complicated and seemingly muddled situation (which, it must be remembered, still appeared in 1787 to be perfectly defensible and intelligible to the majority of those Frenchmen who played any part in public affairs) is to say that the monarchy had come to embody the innovating, active elements in the French constitution, while the mass of rights, which was its most striking and familiar aspect to those who lived under it, embodied its conservative force and inertia. France was not unusual in this respect, for several eighteenth-century monarchs tried to innovate and reform in the teeth of their subjects' opposition, usually with the aim of generating revenue to spend on foreign policy. Tradition, geography, and the international circumstances in which they found themselves, all made this course increasingly attractive to French ministers in the 1780s. Some of them wanted to do other things, too. In a country containing, perhaps, more literate people and an intellectual élite with more of a taste for speculative thinking than any other, and in an age productive of reforming projects, much was said about reconstructing law and the judicial system on more rational lines or of introducing a greater measure of religious toleration, encouraging agriculture by permitting free trade in grain, or taking better care of the poor. But all such things (and many more suggestions had been made) antagonized some people and often they antagonized those with important powers of resistance, respect for legal rights being what it was.

The *parlements* often led and expressed this resistance and for a long time it made them popular. Yet by 1789 they were reviled for it. This came about because of an important change in the attitude of many who comprised the élite of French society towards the principle upon which the whole old order rested and the *parlements* defended—legal privilege. It had been so pervasive and so generally accepted for so long that the change is hard to explain. Privilege was not reserved to a narrow class; the relatively well-off groups which dominated French life and enjoyed most of its rewards in the 1780s embraced at one end the formally noble and at the other bordered on an ambiguous social zone. From this vague, twilight area petty legal officials were constantly emerging to take lowly but definite places on the lowest rungs of official life, while, on its further side, successful craftsmen were entering it from their workshops. Movement within the world of non-manual workers was continuous and progress upwards was by no means of baffling difficulty. Big social leaps by individuals were rare, it is true; it usually took family effort for two or three generations to make remarkable improvements in social position within the dominant class (even the newly ennobled or *anoblis* were still three generations away from recognition of their hereditary nobility). Still, once money had been accumulated (and this was overwhelmingly the most important consideration at each step in the process) the purchase of an office which itself conferred personal nobility, or of a fief whose possession gave the position and title of *seigneur* even to non-nobles, were among the most common and recognizable steps by which families moved upwards. They did so, moreover, in a structure of astonishing complexity. The ambiguities of status which proliferated within it facilitated movement and further increased the diversity of the French élite, which was undefined by function or economic role. Eighteenth-century lawyers often found it hard to decide at what point men who owned fiefs, who were referred to as 'noble' by courteous neighbours and might have appropriated titles which those neighbours habitually employed, or who lived in decent style and comfort and might possess offices conferring personal nobility—or have close relatives who did—actually crossed the line of hereditary nobility towards which all well-disciplined and well-off French families pressed so purposefully. And even within the legal category of hereditary nobility, confusion could be almost as great once questions of rank and precedence had to be weighed. There were poor nobles and rich nobles, those who lived contentedly in the provinces and those who cut a figure at court. There was no more clear distinction of function or wealth (except perhaps at the very top of the tree, where the peers of France and the princes of the blood royal clustered in lonely eminence) shared by them all, than there was any line between them and the upper ranks of the well-to-do but commoner families pressing to join them.

Most of this socially dominant class owned some real property; this was the essential destination of money made elsewhere. Because of this, and because they aspired to seigneurial, official, or noble status, the whole of this large group had a personal interest in the maintenance of legal privileges of all sorts, and therefore in defence of privilege in principle. Yet, somehow, this élite became divided; its members often found themselves at loggerheads, and in the process some of them turned on legal privilege and began to attack it in the name of juridical equality and practical re-form. When this happened, the true, formal nobility, was in-creasingly isolated and made the scapegoat for what was increasingly seen as an abuse of privilege. How and why it happened is in large measure explained by a financial crisis which in the end led to the destruction of the old monarchy.

Early crises had been surmounted; what had happened by 1787 was that it had become clear that the monarchy was no longer credit-worthy, that it could no longer raise money by taxation or borrowing which would enable it to service a huge burden of debt inherited from the wars it had fought in the previous half-century, and that without a reinvigoration of its finances it was condemned at best to a secondary role in the affairs of Europe. Yet such a reinvigoration was hard to conceive if existing assumptions about French society and government were unquestioned. All previous attempts to accept them as a framework for reform had failed. Yet to discard them was to many Frenchmen in an almost literal sense unthinkable.

At this juncture, the controller-general of finance, Calonne, an ambitious and intelligent royal servant, was prepared to go further than his predecessors. In 1787 he proposed a com-prehensive scheme of reform to re-establish the health of the

State. To plans for economies in administration, debt redemption, and the promotion of internal free trade in grain he added proposals for new taxes, but ones with a new look, specifically directed to cutting into fiscal privileges from which so many benefited. He persuaded the King to summon an 'Assembly of Notables', or great men of the kingdom, which he hoped would approve his plans and give them moral authority when the moment came to translate them into laws which would go before the *parlements* for registration. This turned out to be a mistake. Instead of responding to Calonne's persuasive exposition of the merits of his plan, the Notables—many of whom disliked and distrusted him—seized the chance to attack his policies and demanded accounts of the royal finances which (they believed) would expose his ineptitude and possible corruption.

Calonne was dismissed. His successor proposed a programme of reforms almost as comprehensive and perhaps better conceived, but tried a different tack, deciding to meet head-on any opposition which the *parlementaires* might show. On 8 May 1788, members of the *Parlement* of Paris were exiled after protests against the reform decrees and two of them were arrested on the floor of the court; English precedents from the reign of Charles I were recalled. Unfortunately for the Crown, the moment for a policy of Thorough such as that urged on Charles was already past (even if it had ever existed). There was widespread popular agitation on behalf of the *parlements*. In the uproar much began to be heard of the cry of 'liberty'. It was thus first advanced in the old cause of defence of local rights and personal and corporate privileges by the *parlements* and other local representative bodies— what they sought was liberty from 'ministerial despotism'. The Government, faced with the need to finance a threatening crisis in foreign affairs at the same time as a strike of capital, was more and more embarrassed; the usual sources of short-term credit now dried up completely because of the quarrel with the *parlements*. In the end this led to the fall of the ministry and, more importantly, to the opening of the way to something which few of the *parlementaires* and their upper-class supporters can ever have wanted, a truly radical transformation of French society and the sudden emergence of the issue of privilege in a new form.

The consultation of France

In effect, France was now to be consulted about what she wanted. This was what was meant by the decision to summon the Estates-General (another antique institution, last called in 1614) to meet early in 1789. In this body, the subjects of the King of France were supposed to be represented in their three great medieval 'orders'—the Clergy, the Nobility, and the 'Third Estate', the large and amorphous category comprised by the non-noble laity. They were now to come together to tell the King of the grievances of his people and to concert with him in finding remedies.

This was in one way a huge concession by the Crown— the trend of monarchical policy since the days of Richelieu had been to evade control or scrutiny by representative bodies—but seemed to be the only way to mobilize support for agreed reform which would be irresistible. The ministry turned to the Estates-General because it faced the impossibility of making progress on any other basis. The *parlements* had for some time agitated for the assembly of the Estates-General, it is true, but this was because they thought it would be more effective than their own powers had proved in curbing the despotic tendencies some of them saw in Crown policy. They were soon to be undeceived.

This was because the summoning of the Estates-General as the *parlementaires*—and perhaps most other Frenchmen who thought about such things—envisaged it was sociological nonsense. The legal definition of the three Orders corresponded to social and economic realities of which most were long dead. The social élite which had sustained the agitation of the pre-Revolution was riven in two by the imposition of the out-dated and legal distinction between noble and non-noble; the Third Estate of commoners (*roturiers*) embraced at one end millionaires who had far more interests in common with rich noblemen than with the poorest peasants at the other end of it. The effect was to change the terms of political debate. What had hitherto been going ahead was argument about the content of reforms which would affect all privileged people, the tapping of their wealth being the essential issue. What now opened was a much more bitter questioning of the right of one section within the French élite, that defined by the legal status of nobility, to avoid burdens laid on its non-noble members. These non-nobles were thus driven to quarrel with the nobles whom they resembled in taste, style of life and assumptions, and to ally themselves with poor men with whom they had nothing in common except what was implied in the gothic logic of the lawyers.

This division, it must be said, was not entirely unanticipated. It has been thought that social forces already at work had tended somewhat to sharpen the sense among some of the aspiring and wealthy but *roturier*-born that the achievement of formal nobility was becoming harder. The channels of social ascent seemed to be in danger of silting up. Not all the evidence is available, but it is difficult not to conclude that there was towards the end of the century a growing tendency for the topmost posts in the judiciary, bureaucracy, and the army—all of them potentially of the greatest value and importance to a family making the final stages of its social ascent to formal nobility—to accumulate in the possession of an oligarchy of those who had themselves been making their way upwards towards them for the last century or so. There was, after all, not a limitless supply of such jobs; a feeling grew that access to them was being deliberately impeded as the end of the century approached. Much more wealth seemed to be necessary to secure them than at earlier times. As economic trends turned against those on fixed incomes, such offices became more desirable for purely financial reasons, too. For many reasons, therefore, what some later historians labelled (perhaps exaggeratedly) an 'aristocratic reaction' (it might as well be termed the self-defensiveness of placemen) was sensed by many people who felt frustrated in their legitimate expectations. Thus the decision over the Estates-General was a catalyst, crystallizing antagonisms sensed but not always openly expressed hitherto, as well as the creator of grievances *ab initio*. With that decision, the image many of the privileged but non-noble held of the formally noble came to be dominated by the very special and visible advantages enjoyed by the topmost stratum of society, at whose heart a few thousand noblemen (*les grands*, as they were called) all but monopolized royal favour and access to the fountains of honour and profit which played so vigorously at Versailles.

The same decision put the cat among the pigeons in another way, too, by creating uncertainty about what precisely would happen next. When the *Parlement* of Paris set out its own views about the composition of the Estates-General, recommending that it be managed in the same way as in 1614, the Orders deliberating separately, and represented in equal numbers, the gulf between their views and those of many other Frenchmen became apparent. Suddenly it was realized that while such an Estates-General might hamstring a royal ministry, it would not touch the structures of privilege which the *parlements* had so long defended and which many Frenchmen were now beginning to question. One of the first manifestations of something which can reasonably be termed 'public opinion' was an outburst of attacks in the press on the *Parlement* of Paris.

It is not easy to set out a chronology of the development of ideas, but the winter of 1788 in this way saw the final politicizing of a debate which had been going on in a muddled and ill-defined way ever since the 1770s. At its centre was the clarification of an idea of enormous revolutionary power, that of national sovereignty. Once the notion had got about that the Estates-General had a quite special and superior status, making them different from the other historic institutions of the monarchy, it was quickly said that they could make laws to bind all Frenchmen and could overrule particular and historic privileges. It was a long time before this was generally agreed—even a majority of the members of the Estates-General did not reach this point until well after they met—but it was an idea which offered a means of radical reform: France might find in the Estates-General the equivalent of the legislative sovereignty enjoyed by the parliament of the United Kingdom. This was precisely why so many of the *parlementaires* shied away from anything but the old, delimited, divided Estates-General of 1614.

Eighteen months or so later, an imaginative statesman was to advise Louis XVI to put himself at the head of what was by then a revolution; perhaps that was too late in the day, but it is at first sight strange that the monarchy did not seize the opportunity to lead the Estates-General in a programme of reforms. Instead, royal ministers had long resisted the pleas to assemble them, seemed to accept them more or less in desperation and then left the question of their composition for a long time unsettled and debatable. Two questions were central: the number of representatives of each Order, and the question of whether voting should be by Order—in which case the first two Orders would always be able to outvote the Third Estate and block the way to reform which damaged their privileges—or by head—in which case the way in which the question of numbers was settled was of paramount importance. To capture the allegiance of reforming opinion, and mobilize it in the shape of a strong Third Estate which could override the other two in support of a coherent strategy of reform, now seems an obvious tactic for the ministry and one which, moreover, might have reinforced the authority of the monarchy. Yet this was not attempted.

Instead the royal government dithered, as it was to do time and time again in the next twelve months. The explanation is complicated. At a general level, the monarchy was itself too much a part of the ideology and institutions of privileged France for such a popular and national programme to be feasible. The assumptions and institutions on which it rested presupposed the importance of privilege and the sanctity of the established order. Royal ministers had tried to get the privileged to pay their share, not to question their rights in any fundamental sense. The personality of the King also counted for much; it was the central weakness of the monarchy that in the last resort everything in government rested on the absence or presence of a royal impulse. Louis was temperamentally unlikely to respond to urgings to act positively to anticipate difficulties, and was personally deeply attached by habit and sentiment to the nobility; the first gentleman of

France could not let the other gentlemen down. Finally, the ministry was divided. It had been joined by the Swiss banker and, supposedly, financial wizard, Necker (his appointment had been necessary to restore the confidence of the financiers so that the monarchy could again borrow money); he represented reform, but confronted strong opposition from his conservative colleagues.

The ministry's uncertainty had as a background an atmosphere of growing excitement and deepening distress; after a poor harvest, the winter of 1788–9 was unusually severe and an industrial slump in northern towns was made worse by the political crisis and a recent relaxation of protection against English goods. But debate in the press was all the time raising political expectations; a multitude of specific grievances, collective and personal, were beginning to seem susceptible of removal once the Estates-General met and a benevolent King heard in person the needs and wishes of his people. A few began to think of reforms which went further than anything envisaged when the Estates-General had first been conceded as a way round the financial *impasse*. It cannot be said that many Frenchmen yet wanted a revolution, but many wanted changes which, even though they might see them in very specific and local forms, were likely to add up to an irreversible break with the past.

The decision finally taken by the ministry to give the Third Estate as many members as the other two combined was widely welcomed, though some of the members of the privileged Estates at once protested. Each electoral assembly in due course sent its deputies (as those chosen as representatives were called) to Versailles with statements of grievances (*cahiers de doléances*); some of those from the privileged Estates were accompanied by instructions to the deputies to prevent any further weakening of legal privilege. Yet the *cahiers* showed a broad predisposition among all three Orders to accept the principle of fiscal equality, so that it might have been expected that the shoals on which earlier reform had run aground might be successfully navigated this time. The question of the form in which the Estates-General should conduct its business when it assembled, though, had still not been settled.

The Estates-General finally met on 5 May 1789, a date which many accept as the beginning of the French Revolution. Yet what assembled at Versailles was, as we have seen, one of the great historic institutions of France. The deputies processed to a thanksgiving *Te Deum* robed and dressed so as to mark the distinction of the three orders to which they belonged; when they took their places for the inauguration of their sitting by the King, they did so again as distinct bodies. Here at last was a physical presentation of the latent conflict between privileged and unprivileged which had increasingly come to dominate political thinking.

When the ministry failed to give a clear lead on what the Estates-General should do—in substance, Necker simply expounded at tedious length the financial problems facing the monarchy and invited the deputies to reflect on them—the initiative in this conflict was going begging. It was seized almost at once by some members of the Third Estate who, without knowing it, thus also seized the initiative in the French Revolution. A formal question of procedure, in the matter of the verification of the credentials of the deputies, was turned into a quarrel between the Third Estate and the privileged orders over whether the Estates-General should debate as one assembly, or in three separate bodies. The issue crystallized an argument of huge scope: was France to solve its problems within the old constitution which rested on specific and legal distinctions of status between men, or were Frenchmen to proceed to the construction of a new society and State based on the institution of the judicial equality of all citizens?

The making of the National Assembly

It took more than two months to resolve. Until mid-June there was little sign that the deadlock which had arisen could be broken. Meanwhile, political expectations rose still higher in the country; feelings became more violently polarized and suspicions dissipated the atmosphere of harmony and goodwill in which the Estates-General had met. Distress in the countryside and high prices and unemployment in the towns fed the exasperation more and more Frenchmen felt towards those who were thought to be frustrating a national will to change. They were increasingly identified as the privileged orders and the ministry.

Within the 'Commons' (as the Third Estate quickly began to call themselves) there was soon a majority for the three orders to meet as one body (in which, of course, *roturier* numbers would be likely to carry the day). Their determination hardened, and after the Commons had given themselves the title of 'National Assembly' and claimed the sole right to control taxation, they were supported on 19 June by a majority vote of the clergy in favour of joining them. The nobility protested to the King over such an outrage to the historic constitution. This provoked the first crisis of the Revolution proper. Faced with the determination of the National Assembly (which had been encouragingly afforced further by two noble deputies) the ministry decided to take the initiative. Unhappily for the Crown, it chose the wrong course. A royal session (*séance royale*) of the Estates-General was summoned for 23 June (which was in consequence to be the last day on which this historic institution appeared on the stage of French history). The deadlock imposed by the intransigence of the Commons was to be broken by an exercise of royal authority. A remarkable and in many ways enlightened programme of reforms was announced; among other things, it conceded the principle of fiscal equality. But it had a fatal flaw: it was one more of a series of proposals for change whose basis was the old absolute power of the Crown and there was no reason to suppose that it would be more successful in imposing itself than earlier attempts. To judge by most precedents, something more durable and vigorous than brittle and half-hearted royal initiatives would be needed to coerce the privileged. Though some of them were already deeply suspicious of the ministry, perhaps this was the moment at which the non-noble deputies as a whole lost confidence in it, for the royal session concluded with the command to debate the royal proposals as separate Orders in the old style. It was too late to make the old constitution work. Symbolically, many of those present refused to leave their places when the sitting ended, and continued their deliberations as the National Assembly. The King was unwilling to use force—so they remained. On the following day more of the clergy joined them; so, soon, did more than forty other nobles. On 27 June, Louis reversed his position and ordered the privileged orders to join the 'two other orders'.

Temperamental dislike of violent measures was to explain much of the irresolution showed by Louis on several occasions during the years which followed, but there were other factors at work, too. Cannon might be the ultimate arguments of kings, but it would take time for troops to be assembled to ensure that the dismissal of the Assembly would not be followed by popular tumults. Preparations were set in hand to assemble forces at Versailles and Paris. Such moves were soon suspected; it was taken as a clear sign that the party of conservatism within the ministry had triumphed when Necker lost his post and set off to Switzerland. But the Assembly's attitude was still hardening, too; on 7 July it set up a constitutional committee and two days later added the word 'Constituent' (*Constituante*) to its title; later it was usually to be referred to simply by this word. The deputies knew they had widespread popular support.

Intervention by the people

Necker's dismissal in fact provoked the final spasm of the old monarchy. Agitation grew as soldiers moved into the neighbourhood and city of Paris. Food, above all bread, had become more and more expensive; bread was the backbone of the ordinary Frenchman's diet and hungry men with starving families were easily stirred by talk of plots against them, which they understood, and by political oratory, whose precise bearing they must often have found obscure. Of both there was a plentiful supply in the hot days of early July. Some Parisians decided to arm themselves against the military *coup* they felt was coming: they were heartened by scuffles which led a cavalry regiment to withdraw from the city and by the defection of some of the security forces to the side of the mob. The propertied classes were alarmed both by the crowd and by the spectre of royal reaction; the electors of

Paris proclaimed themselves the municipal government of
Paris (*commune*) and set up a city militia to keep order.

On 14 July, a day on which, in one of those coincidences
so helpful to historians, the price of bread in the bakers' shops
reached its highest point during the year, a crowd appeared
before the Bastille, an old royal fortress used as a prison which
dominated the centre of Paris. The leaders asked the governor
for the arms they thought it contained (they had already seized
others elsewhere); when they were refused, firing began. The
few pensioners who manned the fortress held out for some
hours against a mob growing steadily in numbers and reinforced by deserters from the army. In the afternoon, the
Bastille surrendered. More gave way than its feeble garrison,
and this is why 14 July is a particularly strong candidate for
the title of the day on which the French Revolution began,
and why it later became a national holiday. It was a great
psychological and symbolic turning-point, for it made apparent something that had been true since May (and perhaps
for long before that): the old absolute monarchy of France
was dead. Unless imposed by foreign arms, there could now
be no reversal of the fact that the National Assembly shared
power with the King. Until this moment, the success of the
Constituent had been contingent; its fate depended on the
ability or inability of the monarchy to assemble the armed
forces which would enable it to recover the lost ground. After
14 July, it was obvious that the coercion of Paris would be
a much tougher business than a monarchy dependent for
money on the National Assembly could contemplate. The first
danger of counter-revolution was over. Necker was recalled,
the King wore the tricolour cockade which had become the
symbol of the Revolution and recognized the legitimacy of
yet another accomplished fact. One of his brothers and a
number of other great nobles fled from the kingdom.

France now had a national representative body claiming
to share legislative sovereignty with the Crown and therefore
to be able to traverse vested interests, prescriptive rights,
and established privilege. It had given itself the task of drawing
up a new constitution. This was a great fissure in the continuity
of French history. Yet most Frenchmen seem to have stepped

across it with confidence. Millions of them believed that King and assembly could now work in harmony to bring about national regeneration. Unfortunately, even if they co-operated, both were at this juncture cramped by a paradoxical powerlessness. The old monarchy had relied on a well-tried administrative apparatus, which had already begun to crumble before the news of the Bastille reached the provinces. With that event, its last authority went; men began to look to the Assembly for orders and not to the old royal or elected officials. Almost everywhere, new municipalities, often (as in Paris) consisting of the electors of deputies to the Estates-General, now took over day-to-day administration to fill the vacuum created by the collapse of the royal authority. They set up local militias on which they thought they could rely to defend order against mobs and the Revolution against military reaction. Yet the Assembly itself could not operate the levers of executive power, or stand at the head of an administrative hierarchy, and had no means of giving orders—not that it had at first any great wish to give them, for it saw its task as the making of laws and, in the first place, constitutional laws. France therefore became practically self-governing as she had not been for centuries, and embarked, though she did not know it, on two years and more of un-precedented administrative dislocation.

A loosening of central government's grip on the reins was enormously to influence the course of events, above all because of new uncertainty it generated about public order. The people had on 14 July appeared as a factor in the crisis, but only the people of Paris; the vast majority of Frenchmen and Frenchwomen lived in the countryside or country towns. It is still hard to discern their individuality and differences behind the loose term usually applied to the majority of them –the 'peasants'. By May 1789, many of these people were in a dangerously excited and sometimes desperate mood. Law enforcement under the old order had always been a problem in as much as the countryside was always a violent place. In the circumstances of 1789 it threatened to become un-controllable.

The special danger of the situation of the summer lay in

hunger—for townsmen and countrymen alike, if they were poor. Two bad harvests in a row, cattle disease, and the beginnings of a liberation of the grain trade from its old regulation by price-controls in the interest of up-to-date economic reform, had all helped to push up the price of food. The unemployment in Paris caused by industrial depression was soon swollen further as the uncertainties of 1789 led to the discharging of domestic servants by the better-off; in the countryside the same depression had already months before brought harsh cutting of earnings in areas of cottage industry where spinning and weaving had traditionally made up meagre agricultural incomes to a subsistence level. Grim as his situation might be, moreover, the countryman had to bear this new strain at the end of a long period of worsening in his economic condition. The exceptions in a country so diverse as eighteenth-century France were manifold but cannot disguise the overall implications, for millions of its inhabitants, of a steady growth of population unmatched by an equivalent rise in productivity. The long-term trends had for nearly fifty years been telling against the poor. Real wages in rural France declined for twenty or thirty years before 1789, and price inflation had been felt for about the same time. Even the peasant exploiter of land sufficient to supply him with a cash crop found that it did not protect him against the demands of landlords anxious to put up rents as leases were renewed and to revive old dues and obligations, or against the rising prices of goods he wanted to buy and higher taxes; the lot of the very poor, with nothing to sell except their labour, was truly appalling.

The excitement of the summoning of the Estates-General, the stimulation of the village meetings to manage elections and draw up *cahiers* of grievance and pleas for reforms to be sent to the King must be seen against this background. Agitation inflamed much of the countryside; it seems very likely that a majority of its adult inhabitants had by June a vague but deep expectation of a great change to come, when a good King would act to remove the innumerable specific ills which afflicted them. That expectation was to legitimize acts of violence and illegality all too understandable and even predictable in the economic conditions of the summer. When this happened, the divided dominant class suddenly found itself facing a third force, a popular revolutionary movement (though that term suggests much more unity than it possessed). Its demands, though often very specific and precise to the individuals who formulated them, added up to a complex and incoherent whole, but were, because they were so widespread, likely to prove irresistible if the old regulators of society ceased to operate. In this tangle of purposes lies one of the deepest sources of that puzzling aspect of what came to be called the Revolution, its Janus-like aspect, looking to past and future at the same time, from a muddle of change and continuity.

2

The Revolution as discontinuity
(i) The Constituent

POPULAR violence was a continuing theme in French history well before 1789. In that year, though, it acquired a quite new importance. The action of the Parisian mob and of countless peasants and inhabitants of small towns all over the country made possible a real and unprecedented disruption of old continuities. Without this popular revolution, the Constituent would have had no power. What is more, popular pressure was to continue to determine much of what was done with that power; disorder ran on through 1790, though historians long tended to overlook this fact. This neglect is understandable. The men who made speeches and voted laws were not anxious to advertise their lack of autonomy and it was undeniably true, after all, that what went on at the centre of affairs was of the first importance. Politics—the courting of support and the wheedling of the new interests created by revolution—was to be the key to French history until an effective central government could be re-created. What must not be lost to sight is the simple truth that these politics were made as much by pressures from outside the Assembly as by politicians within, and that among these pressures the most important came from people who looked to it to do something about their grievances and were willing to act for themselves if it did not. Much was expected of the Constituent. The attitudes of its members matured and developed quickly during the events of the summer months, but even at the outset it is probable that there was a majority ready for important change. In the event, the Constituent (which remained in being until 1791) carried out a colossal—a revolutionary— transformation of French institutions and life. Its work is the

clearest instance of the disruption—deliberate and otherwise
—of French history in the Revolution.

Constitutional foundations

The principles on which the reconstruction of France was
based emerged in the early days of the Constituent. They were
later to be embodied in a constitution. The novelty of this
device was remarkable, but not complete: everyone who had
thought about these things agreed that France already had
a constitution under the old order—but many thought it a
bad one, because despotic and irrational, while others who
approved of it could not agree with one another about what
it was or meant in practice. It was a little like the squabbles of
king, parliament, and common lawyers in early seventeenth-
century England: the assumption of a common heritage did
not make it easier to decide what that heritage was. Still,
many of the deputies had been sent to the Estates-General
with requests from their electors to draw up a new constitution
which would regulate a regenerated France, and many of
them were very ready to do this. It came to be felt that such
a document should embody universal principles and they were
in due course embodied in a preamble to the constitution
entitled a 'Declaration of the Rights of Man and the Citizen'.
This was itself novel, but educated Frenchmen had been
talking in terms of such principles for decades; they were part
of the common cant of public discourse and in the main
reflected the humanity, tolerance, and individualism of the
Enlightenment, the rest being supplied by religion, law, or
the American Revolution. It was not difficult to agree on
them. What counted for more in applying them in the
circumstances of 1789 was the relative weight which could be
given by the deputies to particular grievances about the
existing order.

Broadly speaking, both principles and grievances tended
to flow towards expression in terms of two ideas, liberty and
equality. The events of the summer made many more Frenchmen than before believe that formal institutional restraints
on the power of the Crown were necessary if the representatives of the French people were to be sure they could carry

out what they thought were the wishes of those who had elected them—the better-off, that is to say. The Assembly itself, which speedily claimed (and, thanks to ministerial acquiescence, won) the power of the purse, was the first of these checks; the business of elaborating and defining others and of turning France into a constitutional—that is, a limited —monarchy, was to take the next two years.

By the time that was done, much else had happened along the way. Above all, a new equality between Frenchmen was established. The simple fact of the crystallizing of the National Assembly itself had been a big step in this direction; the obliteration of the legal distinction between the Orders had been decisive. It was followed by the abolition (eventually) of all distinctions of legal status between citizens except those conferred on a functional basis by the sovereign nation, or those which recognized the relation of different degrees of wealth to the exercise of political power. All Frenchmen became citizens, equal before the law, with no special disqualifications because (for example) they were born serfs or Protestants, nor special privileges because of birth, office, or membership of a privileged corporation. 'Aristocrat' was one of the first of a whole series of new portmanteau terms of abuse which revivified political discourse. The subjects of the King of France became Frenchmen; no less and no more. By 1790 this was to lead to the abolition of titles of nobility (the deputies of 1789 had not objected to nobility *per se*, but only to the legal privilege attached to it) and later the egalitarian impulse spurred men to wilder flights of fancy, such as attempts to enforce a 'revolutionary' form of speech, for example, which employed the intimate and cordial '*tu*' instead of the more formal '*vous*' (the '*tutoyer*').

Equality before the law in the matter of both fiscal and juridical obligations was a truly revolutionary break with the past and must not be underrated. Frenchmen replaced a traditional way of thinking about society by a different one, already largely accepted across the Channel, which was of startling novelty for them. Hitherto, the inhabitants of France had no common legal status except subordination (in a great variety of ways) to the French Crown. In law their

relations with one another had been particular and unsystem-
atic; they had enjoyed very different rights. Now, they
suddenly became Frenchmen, juridically equal individuals,
all subject in the same degree to a national legislative
sovereign which was in principle restrained by nothing except
its recognition of rights which would belong to all individuals
equally. This was, on any estimate, a sweeping change. It
took place at the beginning of August, and cannot be separated
from another, the abolition by the Assembly of what it called
the 'feudal order' (*régime féodal*).

The August decrees

'Feudalism' and the 'feudal order' are (and were in 1789)
phrases of misleading simplicity though much of what they
meant in practice had been amply condemned in *cahiers* from
the Third Estate. It is still not easy to say just what they
signified. The *cahiers* of many rural parishes expressed with
varying degrees of precision and force the reality of the irritations and exploitation felt especially by country-dwellers at
the hands not only of those who formally owned fiefs, the
feudal proprietors (*seigneurs*), but also at the hands of landlord
and tithe-collector. Not all of these were felt in the same
way, or by the same people. Irritation against 'feudal' relics
which bore lightly on the Frenchman who owned land was
often vocal, but hardly in the same category as the grievance
of the peasant who found the rent-charges of 'feudal' dues
the last straw when added to other exactions he had to bear.
There had been an intellectual current of criticism of
'feudalism' for several decades which had expressed itself
notably in criticisms of seigneurial jurisdiction, but this was
not what mattered in the spontaneous outburst of rural
violence which was vital in propelling the Revolution forward
after the fall of the Bastille. This was a revolt of sheer misery
and it was a misery for which, above all, the *seigneur* was
blamed.

The sequence of events is easier to trace than to categorize.
Disorders arising from shortages of goods or anger at higher
prices had been going on all year. During June and July this

unrest grew more marked still under the stimulus of rumour and news from Versailles. In many places food shortages and high prices made famine seem near; in some there was starvation. Attacks on country-houses and game reserves, and refusals to pay seigneurial dues became common. By mid-July, with the spread of news of the fall of the Bastille, such disorders were widespread in northern and eastern France. A few people were killed, but for the most part violence was directed against property—if they could, the peasants would frighten their lord into accepting their refusal to pay what they owed him—and against the archives which recorded their obligations. The climax came with what became known as the 'Great Fear' (*Grande Peur*), a series of panics which eventually spread throughout France and left few areas unscathed as rumours announced the approach of 'brigands' (perhaps in the pay of the nobles, some thought) and provoked villagers into taking up arms to defend themselves. Often they then again turned on their landlords. This was the worst spasm of the insurrectionary turbulence of the summer.

Naturally, the Assembly felt bound to act. But to fall back on force threatened to deliver it into the hands of the Crown; soldiers would destroy the revolutionary power on which, in the last resort, the Constituent itself rested. The alternative was to concede what the peasants wanted. But this was difficult for a legislature of landlords, since what the peasants were in effect asking for was the abolition of a species of property.

The final outcome was the passage of a series of decrees early in August. The most controversial of these declared the 'feudal regime' abolished. What did this mean? Specifically, it removed many grievances recorded in the *cahiers*—rights of hunting and game, for example, or those exacting payments based on old obligations to use the lord of the manor's mill, or his baking-oven. It meant, also, the end of manorial courts and of the rights of justice exercised by some *seigneurs*, and the disappearance of the obligation of individuals to provide labour on the *seigneur*'s estate, or to pay dues which were in effect rent-charges instead of it. Yet a distinction between obligations of this sort which were 'personal' in that they had fallen on an individual because he lived in a certain place, and those which had fallen on the property of which he was the tenant, was fundamental to the decrees; the first class was abolished outright, while the second was to be bought out. Redemption charges were to be imposed on those who had paid them in the past, to compensate the landlord who had enjoyed them as a part of his income.

This was complicated enough, yet is far from being the whole story of the contents of this crucial body of legislation, or from revealing its full importance. The whole basis of the finances of the French Church, for example, was undercut when tithe (*dîme*) was abolished, but every corporation in the land lost under other provisions of the decrees. As the relevant wording put it, *all* privileges (and not merely those which were fiscal) which belonged to localities, whether towns, provinces, principalities or anything else, were absorbed into the common law now to govern all Frenchmen (*confondus dans le droit commun de tous les Français*). Here was another unequivocal sign that France was to be rebuilt on new juridical principles. Moreover, such changes also implied an eventual rebuilding from top to bottom of the whole structure of local government and administration. It is incontestable that far more Frenchmen were affected in their daily lives by the decrees' abolition of collective privileges than by changes in personal rights.

Yet many of these, too, were embodied in the same legislation. Not only all personal fiscal privilege, but also all restrictions of status on admission to public employment were abolished. The system of buying offices under government (*vénalité des charges*) which had been the bedrock of the administrative system for two centuries also disappeared. Thus what happened early in August was not just the coercion of *seigneurs* into surrendering valuable privileges. (Many of them, in fact, were going to be better off than before under the arrangements now proposed.) The August decrees went beyond this and embodied the outcome of a complicated political deal between many interests. Agreement on them provided a political majority which opened the way to restoring order in the countryside, but also brought about a huge, somewhat disordered, operation of clearing the decks of the gear of an outdated social order. Yet it is as the 'abolition of feudalism' that the decrees are remembered.

To understand their impact and effect in the countryside we must go behind the misleading simplicity of their phraseology. In the first place, it was far from the case that every part of the country was affected in the same way. France in 1789 was not a 'feudal' polity or economy as a medievalist might use that term. Though only a minority of land was held in outright freehold—the technical term was 'allodial' land—that minority share constituted a large amount of the whole and 'feudal' dues did not affect it. Moreover, old forms often masked new reality. Where seigneurial tenures existed in 1789 they rarely implied service; almost always they had a predominantly, and often a purely, commercial significance. Most of the 'feudal' forms abolished in the August decrees were fictions covering a simple reality of cash transactions. A seigneury was seen by most people as first and foremost an entitlement to income. The charges which made up this income could, and did, bear very differently on different parts of France. Not all Frenchmen suffered equally from the seigneurial yoke.

Something must also be allowed for the confusion introduced into discussion of this subject by the blurring of the term 'feudal' by the revolutionary publicists until it became a portmanteau term denoting all aspects of a presumably barbaric past, from the beliefs of the pious to the institution of monarchy itself. This blurring had already begun in 1789. Tithe, for example, was regarded by many peasants as part of the order which was under attack and was referred to by pamphleteers as a 'feudal' relic, though its legal and social basis and impact were quite different from those of the seigneurial payments. The use of the adjective 'feudal' in 1789 to categorize rural life shows how far French institutions had evolved beyond the conceptual world in which they had been defined. The social idea of the nobleman-*seigneur* might linger at the back of the minds of aspiring proprietors, but in 1789 only a minority of proprietors were *seigneurs*, not all *seigneurs* were noblemen, and many noblemen were propertyless. The archaic legal forms of French land law had already had to give way to the realities of the pressures created by the search for a return on investment—by rural capitalism, in fact—and this had led many landlords to much more rigorous exploitation of their legal rights as the eighteenth century drew on. This was why the dues owned by tenants were more than just a symbolic focus of reform; besides always being irritating (because hard to relate to a service rendered) they became particularly obnoxious in hard times—and 1788 and 1789 were very hard.

Difficult though it is to generalize, this provides us with clues to the nature and significance of the rural revolution in 1789. First and foremost, it was a great step—the most important in French history—in the legal emancipation of the soil and those who exploited it. Whatever had already happened within the limits of the old law to make land a commodity like any other, the sweeping away of seigneurial tenures and the reduction of virtually all land-holding to freehold, leasehold, or share-cropping, together with the bonfire of bizarre impositions on tenants (the obligation to use the seigneurial mill or wine-press and pay for it, for example) and all the rest of the gothic survivals of medieval dependence, spelt everywhere the explicit onset of the market economy in the countryside. To this change, others such as the abolition of primogeniture and the introduction of internal free trade (most importantly, in grain and salt) were supplementary, so that the decrees of August should not by themselves be made to bear the whole weight of responsibility for it. They were, nonetheless, absolutely necessary to it.

Large numbers of people, probably a majority of Frenchmen, were directly affected by the changes. Agriculture dominated the French economy, providing most of the national product and more employment than any other sector, and land absorbed more savings than any other form of investment. The political importance of such steps was therefore immense. That so many people had been daily brought into contact with the 'feudal' reality also helps to explain some of the excitement and bitterness aroused by its symbols. Rights of hunting and warren, or the jurisdiction of the manorial court, were psychological as well as economic irritants. The abolition of charges payable to the *seigneur* on a tenant's marriage or death was a real extension of individual liberty and dignity.

Hatred of the old order in the countryside was often and sometimes unjustly focused upon the nobility, just because noblemen were more likely than non-noble *seigneurs* actually to be living there. *Château*-burning and resistance to the exaction of redemption charges showed this for the next two years or so, and so did a trickle of legislation on matters affecting them. The Constituent showed itself willing to forbid family pews in parish churches, battlements on manor-houses, armorial bearings on coaches, liveries, and the use of titles, and, finally, to abolish hereditary nobility itself. This did not mean, though, that its members, for the most part landowners themselves, would willingly condone interference with invest-ment such as was implied by the refusals to pay the redemption charges prescribed in 1789.

If one outcome of the August decrees (like that of other reforms) was their liberation of France for capitalism, another was a re-routing of French life towards nationalism by over-coming its diversity. This is easier to sense than to measure. Regional distinctions remained rich sources of emotional con-servatism and have found expression right down to the present century in the maintenance of picturesque dress and custom for the delectation of the tourist. It is also true that in so far as the Revolution broke down barriers to tendencies already operating in the countryside before 1789 (such as that towards greater individualism), this was a change less violent than some others. Nevertheless, the disappearance of so many intricacies and peculiarities of local tenures and the abolition of local privileges were great steps towards standardization.

The August decrees were so far-reaching that the ways they worked out in practice clearly cannot usefully be con-sidered except in conjunction with many other changes. Even at this point though, it is worth noting any signs of the extent to which they ran against the grain of French society. One was the ultimately successful resistance of peasants to the redemption of property-based feudal dues.

The work of the Constituent

The prising away of some peasants from the neighbours with whom they had for a time allied, which began to show by the end of 1789, was not the only way in which what we may broadly call 'the revolutionary movement' was under strain. The immediate response of the King to the August decrees was to do nothing: he did not give them his sanction, thus raising in many minds for the first time questions about the proper role of the Crown in the legislative process as well as reviving the hopes of those who disliked the new France. Within the National Assembly the divisions of the old Estates-General were still visible in the presence of extreme conservatives from the former privileged orders. Day-to-day events sharpened differences between them and the other members, who were themselves further divided; parties appeared though everyone deplored them and eschewed the name. Meanwhile, the world outside became a politically more complicated place. The middle-class electors and local notables who had complacently watched the paralysis of the possibilities of royal reaction in June and July had already shown concern about the prolongation of the danger of mass disturbances and mob action in the late summer. Much attention was given to the organization of the local militias which had then made their appearance into a new 'National Guard' bearing the responsibility for assuring public order under the direction of the local authorities. Probably the most important cause of disorder in Paris and its neighbourhood during August and September was the continuing high price of bread, but there was all the time a new and growing danger as radical leaders gave more attention to the political struggles of Versailles, where the main business of hammering out the future of France was still going on.

September was dominated by two major concerns. The first was the continuing failure of the King to sanction the August decrees and a Declaration of Rights drawn up by the Constituent, and the second was a debate on what sort of constitutional monarchy France should have—whether, in effect, it should be somewhat like the British. The essential questions were whether there should be two chambers or one and whether the King should have an absolute or a suspensive veto on leglislation. In the end, unicamerality was accepted by an overwhelming majority and the suspensive veto by one of about five to three. This showed that the revolutionary majority itself was now dividing into groups distinguishable on principle (the supporters of two chambers did not want to put the clock back), but also that the majority did not yet believe that the Revolution was safe and feared that it might be reversed in the interests of the old privileged orders.

Some of them also suspected the Court and its influence on the King, though few yet suspected the King himself, for all his slowness in committing himself to the new order. They were not displeased when there was a new popular upheaval. The occasion was the news of a counter-revolutionary demonstration by the officers of a regiment at Versailles on 1 October. On 5 October, a number of Parisian agitators seized the opportunity to deflect (or promote?) a demonstration of women over high bread prices so that it turned into a march on Versailles to lay grievances before the Assembly. Shortly after it left, the National Guards of Paris were assembled to follow the mob. Once at Versailles, the demonstrators obliged the Assembly to send a deputation to the King to ask for action about bread prices; meanwhile, he announced his sanction for the August decrees. The presence of the National Guard was ambiguous; was it to protect the King and Assembly?—and from whom?—or was it to support one against the other? It did not prevent a party of demonstrators from breaking into the palace that night, killing some guards and (the Court later believed) attempting to murder the Queen. This was another turning-point. On the following day the crowd and the National Guard returned to Paris bearing with them the Royal family. Both the Court and the Constituent distrusted the old capital avoided by kings since the young Louis XIV's bitter memories of the Fronde, and sought to resist its pressure. Yet the majority of the politicians also knew that all they had so far won depended on popular violence.

At this time, politicians who can be called moderate dominated the Constituent. When a Parisian baker was lynched on suspicion of hoarding flour in the anticipation of higher prices, they equipped the authorities with a new law on public order. ('Martial law' is a misleading rendering in English of the French *loi martiale*, as this was named; it laid down the conditions under which force might be employed to repress disorder and did not have anything to do with military courts.) They also pushed forward resolutely with the rebuilding of France on the basis of liberty and juridical equality. This has led to the categorization of this phase of the revolution by some as a 'bourgeois' revolution, one, that is to say, which sought to entrench the class-interests of those whom later Marxists called the *bourgeoisie*, the possessors of industrial, commercial, and agricultural capital. Because this social category is difficult to define precisely and even more difficult to identify in the events of the 1790s without deforming the realities and blurring the nuances of French social structure, much ink and passion have been spent debating it. What can hardly be questioned, though, is that whatever the constraints under which they worked and however they thought of themselves (or others thought of them) in the 1790s, the men of the first National Assembly in the end set up institutions suited to market society rather than status society. These institutions tended to liberate intelligence, talent, and capital for exploitation by those who possessed them in a competitive world. In such a world, those who did not possess these advantages would be handicapped—and, just occasionally, more handicapped than they had been under the old order. But as such handicaps were seen as natural, this did not strike enlightened men as unjust.

Several laws passed by the first National Assembly announced the change. Once the crisis of 1789 was over and an adequate harvest had taken the sting out of shortages in Paris, for instance, the Assembly declined to tamper with internal free trade in grain. Its introduction had often been attempted in qualified forms in the last years of the old monarchy; now it was a reality. The destruction of the old internal customs system and the removal of provincial and municipal privileges pointed in a similar direction. So did the removal of corporations which regulated access to and the conduct of various trades, and so did the abolition of privileges accorded to some manufacturers by the old monarchy. In 1791 there followed a law (named after the deputy who introduced it, the Breton Le Chapelier) which forbade associations for the protection of their interests by workmen or employers; it was to remain on the statute book for most of the next century and to be used against the rising trade unions of an industrializing France.

One issue which more than any other crystallized opinion about the shape of a new France was that of who should effectively exercise the national sovereignty henceforth proclaimed as the basis of the French constitution. This lay behind bitter debates about qualifications for the vote and for election to the National Assembly, the first and clearest confrontation between limited and democratic views of the Revolution. At the back of the minds—and sometimes in their forefront—of the majority of deputies was the threat to property which the eighteenth century saw lurking in a democratic franchise. It was an issue which was to distinguish liberals from democrats for the next fifty years and more. In the end, the National Assembly handed legislative power to the propertied. It divided adult male citizens into two classes: the 'passive' (of whom there were about 3 million) did not have the vote, while about 4.25 million 'active' citizens did. One of the qualifications for active citizenship was payment of direct taxes equivalent to three days' wages; higher up the representative structure wealth mattered more, for the franchise was a two-tier one and the active citizens chose electors (about 50,000 of them in all) who paid taxes at a higher level still. Finally, the qualification for political power by wealth was dearest at the top of the structure: only a landholder who paid direct taxes of 52 *livres* a year—the 'silver mark' (*marc d'argent*)—could be a deputy to the Assembly. Both principles and details of such changes were long contested (in the end, agitation against the *marc d'argent* was successful and the final qualification of deputies was reduced—but at the price of raising that of electors) and many of them were not to survive long. Nevertheless, France's next legislature was to be elected under them.

In other ways, too, the Assembly changed France forever. On the ruins of the old administrative and legal structures was built a more rational and coherent apparatus intended at first to decentralize power, but one which proved in the end compatible with a high degree of central control. The old provinces and divisions of royal government, together with the fiscal divisions of the country into areas subject to different taxes, and the division of justice into areas over which different *parlements* had jurisdiction, all gave way to a system of eighty-three new 'departments'. These were intended to provide areas of approximately the same size, as the framework for all the operations of administration and justice. They were to be governed by councils chosen by the departmental electors and below them were three further layers of local government, also governed by elected representatives, the 'districts', 'cantons', and 'municipalities'. There were to be important fluctuations in the amount of practical independence these bodies enjoyed, but French government still operates today substantially within this framework. As for justice, this, too, was fitted to the departmental structure, the whole system being capped with the setting-up of a new High Court. Its lower levels were provided with elected judges.

Though the Assembly was prepared to be radical in building anew it faced a grave problem of public finance which could not wait for considered reconstruction. Without this, there would not have been a Revolution; the revolutionaries had now to solve it. The rationalization and reform (in an egalitarian sense) of the tax system was taken in hand. The principles of attributing the power of the purse solely to the National Assembly and of separating the personal expense of the monarchy from its public functions were easy to agree upon. The problem of public credit might be solved in the long run as people grasped the significance of such steps, and the temporary economic depression of the later 1780s was left behind and the National Assembly showed its ability to regenerate the country. But when all this was allowed for, ready money still had to be found for running the country in 1789.

A suggestion was made (interestingly, by a bishop) that

the nation should make use of the wealth of the greatest corporation in the land, the Church. The Assembly agreed to this on 2 November. This decision was of the greatest importance; not only may it well have made possible the survival of the Assembly, by providing the sinews of government and reviving the public credit, but it also involved the redistribution of a huge slice of the national capital—somewhere between 6 and 10 per cent according to the best estimates—of all real property.

Not all churchmen welcomed the idea; there was talk of spoliation. But some did and opposition was not so strong in principle that it could not be braved. The argument was put forward that Church property was not like other property in private hands; it was really national property which had been held in trust for the purposes of maintaining the structures of religion, but which could be resumed if the State could provide for this in some other way. That responsibility for the stipends of the clergy—a topic on which the *cahiers* had already said much that pointed to the need for reform—would be met by the State was already accepted since the August decrees; this, too, was to have very large implications for the future history of Church and State in France.

In fact, the main problems of the operation at first appeared to be not questions of principle but of technique. How was this enormous mass of property to be handled so as not to impose upon the State intolerable managerial problems and without a collapse of the land market as so much property was sold? The answer was found in the invention of a new financial instrument, a sort of bill of entitlement, guaranteed by the nation. In return for the payment of a sum in cash, French citizens were assigned an interest-bearing bond—the *assignat*—which could be redeemed at its face-value by being used to pay for 'national lands' or *biens nationaux* (as the former properties of the Church were designated) when they came up for auction. Though it was not so intended at first, the government made further issues to ensure a steady flow of money, for *assignats* were in effect bonds backed by real property, whose disposal could be so phased as to overcome the danger of a collapse of prices. It was hoped that this would permit the extinction of the national debt inherited from the old order.

Unwittingly, the Assembly thus gave France a new and paper currency. This took time. The first *assignats* were not all taken up; in part because of uncertainty about the way in which the Church property would be liquidated, in part because they had the high face-value of 1,000 *livres* each. Then came further governmental steps—more and more *assignats* were issued; partly because of this they tended to depreciate; they were issued in smaller denominations; they were declared acceptable for the payment of taxes and later for the acquittal of other debts to the State; they ceased to bear interest in May 1791. A discount market in *assignats* established itself and this stimulated their use as negotiable paper in other transactions. Their original purpose more and more lost to sight, they increasingly approximated to and eventually became currency. The long-term balance of good and evil effects of this has and can be much debated, but it is indisputable that the immediate impact was considerable. The *assignats* financed the Revolution.

The liquidation of the property of the Church meant the disappearance of the greatest single French landowner, though this description might better be rephrased to take account of the immediate and local form in which it confronted Frenchmen: hundreds of the major landowners of France— abbeys, cathedral chapters, nunneries, colleges—ceased to be landowners. The computation of this is still far from exact. Local variations are all-important and make it an unrevealing statement by itself. In many places, a religious corporation was the major landowner; in others ecclesiastical property was insignificant. In the North and East the extent of clerical property appears to have been fairly high, perhaps running from 20 to 40% of the whole; it was much less in the West and South but, of course, this says little about its local impact, because a district might have a very low percentage while one clerical estate could loom large in a particular commune within it. The impact of the change was different, too, in country and town (where a great deal of ecclesiastical property was located). Perhaps even local feeling counted for something; there were good and bad landlords among the clergy as among the laity. All that can be said with certainty is that wherever there was a substantial block of ecclesiastical property, its sale was bound to affect importantly the balance of landholding and property in that locality.

Because of this, the mechanics of disposing of Church property mattered a great deal. In April 1790 the new departmental authorities took over rights of administration from the clergy. They applied rules laid down by the Assembly to ensure simple procedures, good prices and, if possible, sales of assets in economically viable units. This told against selling the property in small lots and therefore against would-be purchasers without much capital, who were further handicapped when co-operative collective bidding with a view to later sub-division was forbidden. Gradually, the system laid down by the National Assembly was infringed by subsequent regulation so that the smaller proprietor had better opportunities, but not before most of the national lands had been sold. Again, the overall effect is hard to pin down without equivocation, but all local studies appear to show that, broadly, national property was bought by, or ended up in the hands of, those who already had property, and somewhat in relation to their wealth at the outset; most of what came on to the market went to the wealthier among those who were already landowners.

Ecclesiastical reconstruction

Meanwhile, financial support had to be provided for the Church. This was only one of several motives for the Assembly to address itself to ecclesiastical questions. An immense amount of encouragement and guidance was to hand in the *cahiers*, which specified numerous targets for reform: absenteeism, pluralism, inadequate stipends for the lower clergy, and the redrawing of diocesan boundaries were among the most popular. The Revolution itself had created other problems besides those raised by the sequestration of ecclesiastical property and the abolition of tithe; the abolition of perpetual vows and corporations, the proclamation of the principle of the liberty of the press, the reconstruction of administration and delimiting of jurisdiction, all had profound effects on churchmen. And behind all these lay an even more fundamental explanation of much of the excitement which was to follow: under the old order there had been literally nothing in French life which did not concern the Church, and that old order was now being set aside at almost every point.

The men who undertook to deal with these problems were neither anti-religious nor anti-Catholic. A few, it is true, were somewhat anti-clerical. But in view of the polemics subsequently generated over the religious legislation of the Revolution, it must be stressed that the men of 1789 did not contemplate the de-Catholicizing of France. Nor were most Frenchmen expecting a major upheaval in life and thought. Historians have recently begun to investigate with new success an old and vexed debate about how 'Christian' France still was, in terms both of observance and mentality, on the eve of the Revolution. Comprehensive answers are still to seek (and may perhaps never be available) but it would be rash to say that France was ripe for a deep rejection of its traditional religious culture in 1789, though this is what some Frenchmen later claimed. Instead, all the evidence points to the acquiescence of the majority of Frenchmen in the continuing belief that France was and should remain a Catholic country, in whose religious life the Catholic church, purged of some of its shortcomings, would continue to play its traditionally preponderant role.

Unfortunately, though those who were most interested in the reorganization of the Church approached it with pious and public adhesion to some such general standpoint as this, putting such a general view into practice could provoke grave and fundamental disagreement. The very idea of a Catholic country had already been compromised even before the Revolution by the monarchy itself when, in defiance of the King's coronation oath, a measure of relief from disabling laws had been granted to Protestants in 1788. Some *cahiers* asked for the repeal of this limited toleration; its further extension, instead, under the provisions of the Declaration of the Rights of Man and the Citizen irritated conservatives and also alarmed them. There was to be much discussion of the exact status of the Catholic religion in France before a new religious settlement was approved and this discussion showed that disagreement lay not far below the surface of the tacit agreement of 1789.

On some aspects of the Settlement there was little contention. Payments to Rome such as annates or Peter's Pence had already been abolished in one of the August decrees. A new and generous scale of stipends which removed old inequities and redistributed income within the hierarchy had been foreshadowed in another, and was fairly easy to agree. The reconstruction of diocesan and parochial boundaries so as to correspond to the new divisions of local government caused more trouble and real difficulties arose for many over the application of the elective principle to the Church; if bishops were to be chosen from among qualified candidates by the civil electors, it was possible that in some cases elections would be determined by the votes of atheists—or, worse still for some churchmen, by the votes of Protestants or Jews. This was another expression of the problem of deciding what was to be the future role of Catholicism in French life, of whether, in fact, the French State was to continue to be Catholic in the old sense of the total permeation of the lay by the spiritual. The settlement's merits in the eyes of many of those who upheld it was that it confined the Church for the future to a spiritual role and removed the social and civic functions it had carried out under the old order.

When all was done, offensive as some churchmen and many laymen who were fervent Catholics found the outcome, the long statute termed the 'Civil Constitution of the Clergy' seemed to stand a fair chance of acceptance by clergy and laity alike when it was sanctioned by the King on 22 July 1790. It appealed to Gallican traditions of independence from Rome and dealt comprehensively with practical problems. Yet it was to prove the most divisive single measure in the whole revolutionary legislation. That was largely because what was represented by its supporters as merely a practical settlement of administrative and financial problems was both far more than that to many churchmen, and was allowed to pose a question of loyalty to the State—and therefore to the Revolution. In imposing an oath of allegiance on the clergy the Civil Constitution became, in English terms, a Test Act. Though this oath was taken by all civic functionaries, it seemed to many churchmen that they were being asked to endorse an Erastian view of the relations of Church and State; probably a majority among them, though they feared that this might be so (or might be thought to be so), relied upon the Pope to set their consciences at rest by saying that they might take it. When, instead, the Pope refused his sanction, the French clergy divided into jurors and non-jurors. The oath became a test of the loyalty of clergymen, both to their parishioners and to the State.

This politicizing of religion was crucial for the Revolution's history. The Church was the only truly national pre-Revolutionary institution; there was a priest—or, at least, there was meant to be one—in every parish, so that in every parish in France the question of the nature of the Revolution and what it meant had now to be publicly debated and explicitly answered by men who could often mobilize weighty forces of emotion and habit in support of whatever stand they took. The traditional loyalties of the local community could be awoken against threats from the outside in a way which would be understood and supported in other communities—and those threats would often appear as the emissaries or representatives of a government seeking to enforce other laws besides those affecting religion. Finally, religion made possible a new mythologizing of the issues of the Revolution in the only language and imagery which was shared by millions of Frenchmen.

The new Constitution

The main business the Assembly gave itself was the writing of a new constitution. It had set about its task systematically, by determining the principles on which one should rest. As this was done, subsequent specific legislation was all related to these principles, so that much of the Constitution was actually operating before it was formally inaugurated as a whole in the summer of 1791.

By that time, those principles themselves bore the scars of Revolutionary events, which had led to increasing and justified distrust of the influences surrounding the King, who was, therefore, never allowed to exercise freely the powers which the Constitution formally conferred upon him. These had provided that he should direct the executive power, while the legislative was retained by the National Assembly, though over its decisions, too, he should have a suspensive veto. It had been intended, that is to say, that there should still be a royal role in legislation. Suspicion of the potential influence of royal ministers in the Assembly had led to their exclusion and the formal separation of the executive and legislative powers at all levels below the monarchy itself. The effect was to make it impossible to attribute responsibility for the acts of the executive (soon regarded with suspicion by many deputies) to anyone except the King. When, in a series of acts, not all of them arising from his own inclinations, the King sacrificed much of his early popular and political support, a legislative power confronted an executive which it thoroughly distrusted with no link between them. By the time that the King came formally to accept the Constitution few people believed that he was sincere in doing so.

Why, then, it may be reasonably asked, did they have him sanction it? The answer to this lies partly in the nature of the new order, partly in political history. The Constitution was the work of the socially dominant. It was explicitly rooted in the defence of property, which was not only declared to be one of the Rights of Man and the Citizen but was the basis of electoral and suffrage qualifications. By the summer of 1791, when the King and his family attempted to break away from Paris and fled towards the frontier flinging behind them a violently worded condemnation of the principles of the Revolution, many deputies still felt that the danger of radicalism if the King were removed was too great, and even that he was indispensable. So he was brought back. This was not the whole story; the compromised King still had many supporters at home and the emigrant dissidents on the frontier would have been only too pleased to foment rebellion to restore him to the throne were he deposed. Work on the final drafting of the Constitution was just coming to fruition and civil war might offer a pretext for Austrian intervention at a crucial moment. All in all, then, it was best to keep Louis. And so the members of the Constituent bequeathed to their successors a monarch in whom they did not believe, but also (they hoped) some chance of preserving the constitutional monarchy of the propertied in which they did.

Yet politically this Constitution had opened Pandora's box. Whatever its restricted economic and institutional foundations, it gave birth to political life in France. The Liberty and Equality proclaimed by the Declaration of the Rights of Man were, after all, very real to men brought up under the old monarchy; a flood of journalism and agitation in the autumn and winter of 1789 showed it. So did the rapidity with which the Constituent Assembly had to come round to imposing restraints upon these principles in practice. Among the defensive responses were the restricted franchise, the law on public order, and growing restrictions on freedom of speech and the press. Yet these did little to check political activity. By 1791, the capital was highly politicized through political clubs. The first had been formed by groups of deputies to the Assembly but some (notably that meeting at the old convent of the Cordeliers, from which it took its name) came to have a real popular membership. The most famous, the 'Jacobin' club (it, too, took its name from its meeting-place) became the centre of a network of affiliated local societies which brought together friends of the Revolution from all over France and which had the distinction of being specifically denounced by the King as an obstacle to good government in his manifesto on departing for Varennes. Here were new institutions created by the liberation of 1789. They explain much of the attitude of the Constituent Assembly as it moved to its close and prepared to hand over the new France to its successor.

3

The Revolution as discontinuity
(ii) The war

ONE radical distinction between the new national assembly which assembled at the beginning of October 1791—the Legislative Assembly—and its predecessor, the Constituent, was their membership: no one sat in both of them. The members of the Constituent had passed a self-denying ordinance preventing themselves from standing as candidates and their successors, therefore, were new men. There were differences in what they really represented, too. The Constituent had emerged from the Estates-General and therefore contained many noblemen and clergy; few of these sat in the new body. With one or two exceptions, the nobles now retired from Revolutionary politics—some of them to active opposition abroad—and the twenty-three clergymen in the Legislative (as the new assembly is usually termed) were supporters of the constitutional church, untypical of their order. The membership of the Legislative well reflected the social ideals implicit in the Constitution under which it was elected. By and large, its members were the property-owners of provincial France, local notables who thought that the Revolution had gone far enough even if (as some of them were to show) they did not trust the monarch and were willing to push him by insisting on measures to which he was opposed. There were no real peasants or artisans among them and not many businessmen. In this respect the Legislative was only in degree less representative of all sorts and conditions of Frenchmen than the elected local government bodies. They, too, were filled with notables, drawn in the main from property-owners and professional men (mostly lawyers) prominent in the local oligarchies of the old order.

The Legislative was, of course, intended to be different from the Constituent in function. It was not there to draw up a constitution and rebuild France. But this is not the explanation of its virtually complete failure to shape French institutions positively in any lasting way. On both French and European history the impact of the Legislative was colossal, but it was indirect. The Legislative made its impact by taking France to war at the beginning of 1792. No single decision so much influenced the course of Revolution both at home and abroad. It had not been intended that it should do so, but the war changed everything. It was the major determinant of all that followed for nearly a decade and its importance can be traced further still. Yet the war was in large measure only a by-product of a long and deepening political crisis which ended in disaster for the Legislative itself and for the Constitution under which it was set up. From their wreckage emerged the first French Republic which, though itself transient, left ineffaceable marks on French tradition and ideology and, through its foreign policy, on European history.

This was much more than the new politicians of 1791 had bargained for. They were largely to blame (if that is the word) but their responsibility must be shared by the monarchy. Already in the summer of 1791, the suspicions entertained of the Queen, Marie Antoinette (who, unhappy creature, for all her follies was also from the start tarred with the brush of an unpopular alliance between the old monarchy and Austria), the conscientious fumblings of Louis (who displayed an obvious distaste for much of what he was asked to do), the unscrupulous abuse of uncertainty about the monarchy's real powers and wishes by the emigrant princes, and the growing feeling that a large number of Frenchmen would support an attempt to reverse the course of events all made many politicians touchy and suspicious. This affected their view of foreign as well as of domestic affairs. After Varennes had brought the final collapse of the King's credit, a declaration issued by the King of Prussia and the Emperor of Austria almost at once seemed to demonstrate that international opposition to the Revolution was indeed allied to an internal one focused on the Court. In fact, the Declaration of Pillnitz (where the two rulers had met) had much more behind it than this. Nevertheless, it soured the atmosphere at the outset for the foreign policy of the Legislative and threw further psychological obstacles in the way of co-operation between Crown and assembly.

Yet when functioning normally, French constitutionalism was supposed to rest upon co-operation between a royal executive and a representative assembly. Radical politicians nonetheless exacerbated the latent conflict between the two by promoting legislation about emigrants and non-juring priests which the King found violently offensive. He used his constitutional veto against the latter. Such episodes widened the gulf between King and politicians and strengthened his resolve to use such powers as were available to him. Yet he was less to blame than either his Queen or his emigrant brothers and their hangers-on for elaborate and well-known (though clandestine) encouragement of a foreign intervention which might restore the old order, or at least the power of the monarchy.

There were soon many pro-royalists, both at the centre and the periphery of affairs, who were willing to welcome a war for the chances it promised of a restoration of royal authority, either through defeat by foreign arms or by use of the new powers the royal executive would be likely to enjoy once armies were mobilized under its command. They were not, moreover, the only ones who thought that a war might promote partisan political aims. Besides those who genuinely feared an attempted restoration by the Austrian army, some radicals thought a war would settle the monarchical question by forcing the King to commit himself clearly for or against the Revolution, and still others thought that it would bring them prestige and power as early advocates of it; they assumed, of course, that its outcome would be victory. Thus the deepest causes of the war may be said to have lain in the convictions of men of many different outlooks that the causes they believed in—and sometimes their own personal interests—would be better served by war than by anything else.

During the winter the crisis deepened and the fear of

internal reaction grew. It was fed by the knowledge that large bodies of emigrants were gathered on the eastern borders of France under the command of the princes, waiting to enter the country under the aegis of foreign rulers, whose armies would do the serious fighting to restore the Crown's power. In fact, neither the Emperor nor the King of Prussia (who were the only two serious candidates for this role) wished to do this. Nevertheless, the emigrants were the link between the real and formal causes of the war. After being persuaded to sanction increasingly severe legislation against them, the King finally agreed to an ultimatum to the Emperor calling upon him to dissolve the assemblies of emigrants in the territories adjacent to France. These were not in fact Austrian, but were part of the Holy Roman Empire, and, therefore, territories belonging to princes who were the Emperor's vassals; somewhat disingenuously, the Legislative assumed that the feudal tie of dependence was a real one and in due course when France received no satisfaction, it justified a declaration of war on the 'King of Hungary and Bohemia' rather than on the Holy Roman Empire.

Thus, in the end, the war was both formally and really the outcome of domestic politics. But it brought no such swift resolution of political problems as had been hoped by its advocates. Instead, it exacerbated them. The declaration of war on 20 April was followed by a disastrous month during which a French offensive in Belgium collapsed after a few days; French troops ran away in the face of their enemies, one unit murdering its general, and the King's commanders finished by advising him to make peace at once. The situation was desperate, though not in quite the way the generals thought (for the Austrians were distracted by events in eastern Europe and had no wish to invade France); soon a general who was the 'hero of two worlds', Lafayette, was planning to march on Paris with his army and play the role, perhaps, of the 'new Cromwell' so feared by radicals. His own view of his task, it must be said, was rather that he should be a Monk, restoring the constitutional monarchy as it should have been according to the ideals of the men of 1789, with a royal government and parliament independent of the new obvious pressure from the radicals and their supporters in the clubs and streets of Paris.

The long crisis finally came to a head in the summer of 1792. Defeat encouraged well-founded suspicions of treachery but also produced near-panic; all that had been won in the Revolution was endangered if the Austrians advanced on Paris. Economic conditions there had much worsened as war-time demand soaked up supplies and sent up prices already rising because of the collapse of the currency; gold and silver became scarce and the *assignat*'s value collapsed as the constitutional monarchy which was its guarantor seemed to totter in the balance. Harsher times made easier the radicalization of the Paris 'sections'—the divisions into which the city was organized for local government—and clubs which had begun after the King's abortive flight. Louis' attempt to rid himself of ministers whose supporters in the Assembly distrusted him led to a great demonstration on 20 June, when hundreds of armed Parisians broke into the royal palace of the Tuileries, forcing him to wear the cap of liberty and to drink to the health of the nation. The anniversary of the fall of the Bastille was drawing near; if it was to be celebrated as it had been in earlier years, arrangements had to be made. The King agreed that contingents of National Guards from all over the country should come to Paris for the celebration. When they came, they proved, like the militant leaders of the Paris sections, no longer willing to support the monarchy.

Its time had run out. When Louis attended the 'feast of the federation' on 14 July, he was watched in silence by a hostile crowd. At the end of the month, petitions began to come in to the Legislative demanding his suspension from office. The tension mounted. It was clear that an insurrection was in the offing and it came on the morning of 10 August when the Tuileries were attacked by National Guards and a mob of Parisians. After taking refuge with his family in the chamber of the assembly, Louis gave his last order as a constitutional king (and perhaps his only one in the entire Revolution which was wholly indefensible) that the Swiss Guards, who had until then successfully defended the Tuileries, should cease fire. They did, and many of them were massacred in consequence.

Thus came to an inglorious end one of the great monarchies of Europe. It was formally abolished on 21 September, but 10 August was the real end. It was also—as was soon apparent—the end of the Legislative Assembly, of constitutional monarchy in France until 1814, and of the constructive phase of the Revolution. Very little of what was created in the next few years was to last, except in the form of enduring scars and memories.

The Convention

There followed a crucial phase, temporary but intensive, of disruption and uncertainty while the fate of the Revolution seemed to hang in the balance. Over it presided the third national assembly, a 'Convention' elected in September 1792 to draw up a constitution for a French republic; this body remained in being until 1795. In the same September the spectacular massacre of a number of prisoners held in Paris jails, among whom were many clergy, announced a new legitimation of popular violence and provided martyrs for the cause of reaction. Subsequent events were interpreted by opponents of the Revolution in terms of a mythology of deliberate religious persecution. This had deep roots in fears engendered by the anti-clerical propaganda of the Enlightenment, had been matured by the debate on the Civil Constitution and the subsequent bitterness provoked by the oaths, and was now crowned by the massacres.

The history of the Convention falls into three phases, a struggle between politicians lasting until the end of May 1793, the negotiation of a crisis of domestic and foreign war by an increasingly authoritarian and centralized government over the following year, and finally the slackening of the rigours of this regime and the piloting of the Revolution into less choppy waters where the Convention could at last accomplish its constitutional task and hand over power to the authorities of an organized republic.

The achievements of the Convention were very great; they preserved the Revolution when it might have gone under. Yet they were triumphs of expediency and survival, rather than of principle and construction. Little that the Convention founded lasted very long, though it guaranteed the survival of much done by the Constituent which might otherwise have perished. One of its longest-lasting innovations was the Revolutionary Calendar, and this provides a good symbol of the gap between the aspirations it awoke and the extent of its success. In 1789 some people had optimistically begun writing on their letters 'Year I of liberty', but the practice had not caught on. Under the Convention, it became legally obligatory to use a new calendar in official correspondence, though this was not until the year I (which was supposed to have begun with the meeting of the Convention itself) was over. The new calendar lingered on, last surviving on French coins, until abolished by Napoleon, well into the Empire. It had never had much support among the public at large. No doubt overwhelmingly the most important reason was the sheer inertia of habit and known ways; twelve new names of months based on meteorological or horticultural allusions and the abandonment of such old, familiar landmarks as Easter and Whitsun required a major adjustment in personal behaviour. So fundamental a transformation of familiar patterns of thought and behaviour as was implied could not have been imposed successfully by any eighteenth-century government unless there had been advantages in a new calendar capable of overcoming these powerful forces. But in addition to this, the change awoke positive hostility. One of its aims, after all, was the reduction of the number of the holidays in the old Christian calendar. The heart of the matter was a new ten-day week (*décadi*) which meant a sharp reduction in free time, since Revolutionary sabbaths would only come round every ten days instead of every seven as did the Christian. The rationality and simplicity of the new scheme (twelve regular months, each of thirty days divided into three ten-day weeks, with five—or six—extra days at the end of the year) was not enough to prevail over such objections. From the outset, popular disregard showed itself in many places in the continued observation of the great Christian festivals.

Much of the Convention's legislation, like this, went beyond the limits of what many of its own members would have thought prudent, let alone desirable, in normal times. But the times were far from normal. In the autumn of 1792 France faced defeat in the field, economic privation at home, a sudden and ferocious embitterment of the internal political struggle, and spreading disturbance as the ecclesiastical legislation of the previous year took hold. Almost none, if any, of the members of the Convention (the *conventionnels*) wished to put the clock back in the sense of giving up any of the ground gained by the first two assemblies. But the Convention contained many members like those of its predecessors, middling men, property-owners who would have been happy to see no further revolutionizing of France had they not been impelled to tolerate more radical steps by the danger in which the country stood and harried by the political forces struggling to control and intimidate them. They had to bend before a new popularization of politics which, in its local expressions, was often imposed by force on their more reluctant contemporaries in the echelons of local government.

Crudely, we may simplify the political struggles by saying that the radical political current called 'Jacobinism' determined the Convention's course and attitude from within, while the decisive factor outside was the pressure of the best-organized political movement inside Paris, that of the more radically-inclined sections, those dominated by militant revolutionaries. This was less a sudden irruption than the climax of an insurrectionary wave whose first manifestation went back to the Bastille and whose major achievement was the overthrow of the monarchy. Active politicians sought in debate to persuade, delude, bully, frighten, or charm the majority of *conventionnels*, but did so themselves under the pressure of such outside forces, whether they sympathized with them or feared them.

The decisive party struggles were fought out between two groups of Jacobins in the winter of 1792–3. One came later to be called the 'Gironde' (because some of its most prominent speakers represented the department of that name), but its members were also called 'Brissotins' or 'Rolandists' after two of their leaders. This is significant; they were not a party with a programme but a relatively small group of individualists who could nonetheless co-operate and sometimes persuade other *conventionnels* to follow them because of fears that the courses into which their opponents were leading France favoured a dangerous radicalism. In particular, they feared the Paris extremists and the influence they exercised through the sections and the popular clubs; they believed the independence of the Convention was compromised by it. They were certainly Jacobins, identified with republicanism and members of that political club, but it is not splitting hairs to say that this was only a matter of formal definition. Jacobinism as a national phenomenon had by 1793 passed under the influence of those in the Convention who sat together in a group called 'the Mountain'; these were the *Montagnards*. The prevailing tone and opinion in the Jacobin club of Paris and many of the provincial societies was more violent and extreme than the Gironde accepted and was in sympathy with the *Montagnards*. It may be that 'Jacobin' radicalism in many instances only represented a willingness to set aside constitutional constraints in order to save the country, rather than any deeper and more pondered aims, but this was already too much for the Gironde.

In the end, reluctantly and half-heartedly, but under the pressure of an insurrection, the Convention set aside the moderate opponents of the *Montagnards*, placing their leaders under house arrest at the beginning of June. This made the most decisive break to date with the constitutional theory of the Revolution, in which nothing was more sacred than the person of a representative of the sovereign people. Some have called it a 'third' revolution (that of 10 August 1792 being the second). The Convention was, in fact, feeling the same pressure from outside which had been felt by the Legislative and had destroyed that body in the end, and this pressure had the same roots—hardship among the poor, the fear of defeat and betrayal, and a suspicion of treachery in high places.

The *coup* which gave power to the *Montagnard* leaders heralded and in part precipitated the worst crisis of the whole Revolution. The news from Paris was the final straw to some provincials already worried by what was happening there.

By August, sixty departments were formally declared in a state of insurrection while, at the same moment, France was being invaded from north and south. Things were, it is true, not everywhere equally so grave. Few local authorities actually went so far as to co-operate with the invader; this happened at Toulon, though, where a British and Sardinian force was given possession of the city. At Lyon the former loyal Revolutionary administration had already been ousted by a political campaign in the sections of the city (the same thing had happened at Marseilles) when the murder of a local Jacobin leader provided a Revolutionary martyr and made the second city of France appear a nest of counter-revolutionaries. In other places, municipal authorities limited themselves to proposing that military expeditions (which they then found that they could not mount) go to Paris to protect the Convention or to interfering with and some-times detaining agents of the central government. In many more areas, all that happened was that loyal officials and a handful of local militant Jacobins found themselves virtually isolated among unfriendly populations who might well turn on them if the situation got worse; even if they were not in such danger they often found that they could only enforce the decrees of the Convention by military expeditions into the countryside.

The worst problem by far was in the western departments, where the rising called the 'Vendée' had begun in March in the coastal departments just south of the Loire. It had been detonated by the attempt to enforce conscription, but like insurrection elsewhere was fed by a variety of sources. This was at once the strength and weakness of the various opposition movements which, misleadingly, were seen as one in the crisis of 1793; they were omnipresent, but divided in aim. In some areas they drew on roots in the very deep past—the antagonism of Protestant and Catholic in parts of the South, for example. Some were based upon divisions almost as ancient between classes, localities, occupations, and between town and country, or consumers and producers. Everywhere such antagonisms were inflamed anew by the increasing ferocity of religious (and, in the end, anti-religious) legislation, and by the spreading interference of central government in areas and matters where interference was unwelcome. Usually, the government could certainly rely for support only on local militants and extremists for whom there could be no going back; this, of course, made the policy of government look much more ideologically coherent than it in fact was, delivered it in a measure into the hands of the extremists, and generated new personal bitternesses in societies more and more divided. After the fall of the monarchy, there was little of the Revolution which most Frenchmen could agree in wanting to preserve except the land-settlement, whose final shape was still unfolding but which had its heart in the abolition of 'feudalism' and the dispersal of Church lands. This left wide scope for disaffection, but it was to prove enough to make reunification possible as the danger of defeat began to seem real.

Most of those men who opposed the regime in the early summer of 1793 certainly did not want to jeopardize the Revolution. Yet they were bitterly attacked by the *Montagnards* and were accused of 'federalism'. The phenomenon of 'federalism' and the 'federalists' is an obscure one largely because these words became general terms of abuse (like 'aristocrat' earlier in the Revolution). Federalism had been declared a capital crime at the end of 1792, but not many of those worried by a centralization of government under a Convention supposedly dominated by the Paris mob really questioned the proclaimed unity and indivisibility of the Republic. The substance of federalism was negative, a sense in some important provincial towns that the *de facto* local independence they had enjoyed since 1789 was in danger and that one consequence might be the imposition on them of radical social policies which even the Convention itself might not really want. This sense had hardened steadily; it first manifested itself in proposals after the September massacres that a guard be sent from the provinces to protect the Convention from the mob, and deepened as Parisian violence forced first the concession of price-control and then the purging of the Girondins.

Federalism, unlike the *Vendée*, was almost always

militarily insignificant, but this did not make it less frightening; the *conventionnels* were all too aware of their weakness as they faced what they took to be treason in the major provincial cities. This only threw them back even more than ever on the Parisian sections and their leaders and made it easier for them to swallow the myth of a special Parisian role as guardian of revolutionary purity through the direct democracy of insurrection. In the provinces themselves, federalism, though soon contained, left behind another layer of local vendetta and a new set of winners and losers to quarrel in years to come.

Royalism undoubtedly exploited federalism, but was not the same thing. Conscious counter-revolution did better in the countryside, and it could draw on resistance to conscription and religious loyalty. Counter-revolution had a ready-made social base wherever a non-juring priest retained the loyalties of his flock, even if he was driven into hiding or exile. The intruded 'constitutional' priest represented a threat to the community, the representative in a usurped pulpit of a government which requisitioned crops for the benefit of townsmen, conscripted young men to the army, and interfered with the peasant proprietor's newly won freedom to exploit his holding solely in his own interest.

Important though religion was the great catalyst of counter-revolution had been the war. Its demands in men and supplies transformed the situation of the countryman. The fears of reaction which it generated lay behind the fierce legislation against non-jurors and 'fanatics', as those who publicly adhered to traditional Catholicism were called by extremists. Enforcing such laws gave more power to local hotheads and cranks who could be trusted by the government because of their commitment, but who unwittingly fanned the flames of counter-revolution by their abuse of their authority. They helped to swell the ranks of the martyrs of the counter-revolution. The priests who had died in the September Massacres had been followed in a few months by a royal victim; Louis XVI had been tried and executed in January 1793. Gradually, the counter-revolution turned into a crusade, gathering all sorts of curious and individual causes under the banner of Christ and King, especially in the West. There, the countryside favoured the rebels' operations. Even when the *Vendée* proper had been contained, the wildernesses of Britanny and the Norman *bocage* harboured *chouans* (as they were called), and there was always the hope of British naval support on the coast. The appearance of a Norman nobleman putting into practice skirmishing skills learnt in the American War of Independence should remind us that ideological inspiration and financial cost may not be all there is to notice about its effects on French history.

The struggle for the Revolution's survival

Even those *conventionnels* who sensed ideological triumph in the establishment of Revolutionary Jacobinism in power in June, and who may have hoped to legislate further fundamental change into French life, had immediately to subordinate everything to the pressing need to survive. Recovery in the field had to be won by building new armies and purging generals thought incompetent or unreliable; the second was not difficult but the first required much more government. Conscription was the key; it tapped the French manpower potential which was later to carry the armies of Napoleon to success. But until conscription worked effectively (it was never to work perfectly), new formations were extemporized by brigading national guard battalions with regular battalions while volunteer drafts were used to fill out the old line regiments (the *amalgame*). Then there was the problem of supply; this required not merely the organization of production, purchasing, and requisition, but interference with the economy at large to offset the effects of inflation and shortages of important materials.

This was the main route by which the Convention was drawn into the effort to administer and politicize France as never before. But it was not the only force at work. There was the pressure of the internal opposition in all its variety; it might owe much of its own force to dislike of central government, but to cure it meant a further dose of the disease. On the other side of the Convention there was the pressure of the Parisian revolutionaries who seemed to wish to drive forward the politicians to more and more socially radical measures. The Convention could have been ground to dust between two millstones, counter-revolution and extremism. It saved itself and the Revolution by making concessions to the Parisians which kept their loyalties just long enough to fight off the worst dangers. They were not concessions which would last.

The Parisian militants liked to term themselves '*sansculottes*'. This effectively untranslatable term was a designation of affection and admiration; originally, it signified those who wore trousers and not the knee-breeches of polite society (and were therefore clearly men who worked with their hands). In this sense, it is doubtful if there was a single *sansculotte* in the Convention, though there were a few who worked with their hands and some who shared the *sansculottes*' radical aspiration. But *conventionnels* did not wear trousers.

Sansculotte became one of the most widespread and evocative revolutionary terms, decaying as it did into a canting evocation of revolutionary virtue with regard to anything the user of the term approved. The *sansculottes* of 1792–4, though, can be defined more precisely than this. They were a specific Parisian group with particular aspirations they wished to advance by bringing pressure to bear upon the Convention. It is not mere pedantry to point out at the outset that they were men. Women who attempted to find a place in the *sansculotte* ranks which went beyond rhetorical expressions of solidarity, or the traditional roles of women in giving a special fervour to public demonstrations and attending to the warrior's repose at other times, received short shrift. They were for a time to be seen at some club and section meetings, but did not lead them. The *sansculotte* by no means envisaged the total overturning of the social order attributed to him by the most alarmed of the reactionaries.

Another restricting qualification: the *sansculotte* was a key figure in Parisian politics only in certain sections of the capital. These were those with a popular and artisanal character based on the concentration in them of certain trades and crafts differentiating them from the richer, more purely residential districts (there was, of course, no industrial section, in the modern sense of that term, where large factories grouping hundreds of workmen into what would later be termed an industrial proletariat provided the bulk of employment). The ideal *sansculotte* was the political activist who attended the clubs and assemblies in such sections and kept a close watch on his neighbours' revolutionary temper and the conduct of his elected authorities. Yet this was only the ideal; the demands of earning a living and of the private affairs which make up the most important part of any sensible man's life meant that most of the typical *sansculottes* could not keep up a political role of such intensity for long periods. They did so, nonetheless, for months on end when particular dangers seemed to call for it. As most of 1793 was like this, this was the greatest period of *sansculotte* influence.

This influence was deployed in the support of social rather than of political ideals, though it was central to *sansculotte* thinking that the republic, popular sovereignty (expressed if necessary through insurrection), and equality before the law (and all other positive gains of 1789) were not to be questioned. Liberty was somewhat different; since times were dangerous, it must not be so indulged as to favour counter-revolution. In any case, the concern of the *sanculotte* was the defence of collective liberties rather than of the individual. He tended to talk more about equality, and to this word gave a meaning more extended than did those who admired the market society legislated into existence by the Constituent. In this respect, the *sansculotte* could be very conservative, anxious to regulate the prices of commodities of daily use in accordance with the popular morality inherited from the old order and, as a result, asking for legislation which would have been perfectly comprehensible to the old royal government, careful as it had been of particular and corporate interests. He distrusted the rich because he thought they might not like a revolution of political equality, but did not question the institution of private property. This was the political economy of the master-craftsman and small shopkeeper, social types frequently found in the ranks of the *sanculottes*. The confused impression most of us have of a more radical and more broadly-based political force, representing a poorer stratum of society is based (in so far as it does not rest upon romantic literature) upon the fact that the *sansculottes* were willing to go far, very far, under the stimulus of immediate and obvious danger to the Revolution and that their name and style were eroded when the poor infiltrated the clubs and sectional assemblies.

The interplay of Parisian pressure with other forces explains the policies sanctioned by the *conventionnels* to meet the national emergency. For a time, they attempted to work through an inherited structure of ministerial responsibility to the Convention, but events drove that body's leaders to centralize executive decision in their own hands. Almost unthinkingly, the Convention became the apex of an extemporized system of government, at first fragile and uncertain, whose apparent coherence and undoubted achievements were in the end to provide the world with a model of dictatorial centralization. It was called by its creators 'revolutionary government' (*gouvernement révolutionnaire*), but because of its coincidence in time with other manifestations of France's revolutionary vigour and because of a prevalent violence and (perhaps more important) rhetoric of violence, it has long been better-known as the 'Terror'.

'Revolutionary government'

'The provisional government of France is revolutionary until there is peace' are the opening words of a decree of October 1793. It laid down principles under which France was to be governed for the next year or so. They establish a crucial point; revolutionary government was known to be extraordinary, emergency government, extemporized to meet the need of navigating the rapids of a life-and-death crisis for the Republic, not government striving to transform society. Its antithesis was constitutional government, the suspension of which meant removing, among other things, the guarantees of personal liberty enshrined in the Declaration of the Rights of Man and the Citizen (to which, with small modification, the Convention had proclaimed its own adherence in a constitution approved as recently as in the summer of 1793, but never put into practice).

In December there followed the law of the 14 *Frimaire* (as it is known from its dating by the Revolutionary calendar) whose aim was to organize the chaos of extemporized administrative and governmental practices and institutions. In the process it created new ones and reallocated power among those that existed. It sought to draw in the reins of government and to regain the initiative for the Convention and the committees entrusted with the oversight of different branches of executive government. In the turmoil of mobilization, the raising of supplies and the containment of civil war, the extremists had made the running because they could be trusted to remain true to the Revolution. The decree of 14 *Frimaire* was from one point of view an attempt to curb them once the worst of the danger was past, the invader repelled, and the crisis of the civil war contained. The government then felt safe enough to take its embarrassing supporters in hand. The law was a reactionary document, that is to say, unless you thought (as it was not unreasonable to do so by the beginning of 1794) that the activities of extremist revolutionaries actually favoured counter-revolution.

To understand the law, the institutions it sought to regulate must be the starting-point. Under pressure from below, the Convention had given great powers, for example, to the *comités de surveillance*, or watch-committees, whose task was the general oversight of officialdom, the execution of laws, and public security and order at a local level. In many places these virtually superseded the formal apparatus of local government and they were usually dominated by the local patriotic clubs, the extreme Jacobins. They were given important new tasks every time the Convention passed fresh repressive or regulative laws. The stiffening, to the point of persecution, of the laws against refractory priests was one example. The operation of the Law on Suspects, under which, before the end, over 300,000 people were to be imprisoned, overlapped with this. The holding of Revolutionary festivals, and the supervising of laws against hoarding or cornering foodstuffs were yet other concerns of these committees, and so was the

working of the conscription. And, finally, there was the concession in September 1793 (along with other changes which
register that this was the lowest point of the Convention's
freedom of action in the face of a threat of a new popular
rising in Paris) of more effective price-regulation, the law of
the *Maximum*, an attempt to cure inflation and shortage caused
by speculation at the same time, by fixing prices. Conceded
without teeth earlier in the summer, it was to be made to
work after September by force.

This range of activities offered ample opportunity for
personal vendetta and high-handedness. The local Jacobins
could fall back upon powerful means of intimidation. Offen-
ders were sent before the local Revolutionary tribunals, courts
whose formal briskness of procedure was rendered even more
of a fiction by the political commitments of their members
and their willingness to cut corners to ensure a conviction
from which the accused would pass to guillotine or firing-
squad. The security forces to back this up were the local
National Guards, but because of the civil war and the need
for the army to maintain its supplies, they were often backed
up in 1793 and 1794 by regular soldiers. They carried out
the domiciliary searches and sequestrations of foodstuffs and
supplies which were essential to the working of the war
economy. There were also other bodies, so-called 'Revolutionary armies' (the *armée revolutionnaire* of Paris had been
authorized by law, but others were spontaneously generated
in the provinces) which undertook the tasks of assuring the
supply of food to towns from unwilling agricultural areas and
extended their license from requisitioning to pillage, sacrilege,
the bullying of priests, and the terrifying of country girls.

Over this complication and confusion the Convention was
theoretically sovereign. To its authority there was only one
theoretical limit: the right of popular insurrection, which some
proclaimed as sacred, and which had been demonstrated so
many times since 10 August, which virtually all the politicians
distrusted, and which divided opinion in the country more
each time it was used. It gave the last word always to a
minority, the Parisian *sansculottes*, among whom the belief
was widespread that Paris—the only French city of a half-

million people—had a special moral and political role in the Revolution as the spokesman of the nation; this remained a dogma of French radicals for the next hundred years. Yet in spite of the shadowy and menacing right of insurrection, the theory of the concentration of authority in the national representative body was never abandoned. It was expressed in the working of central government, where ministers reported to committees of the Convention. Among these, emergency conditions gave especial and growing importance to two, the Committee of Public Safety (*Comité de Salut Public*), which had general oversight over policy, and the Committee of General Security (*Comité de Sûreté Générale*), which controlled the working of police and intelligence operations. The theory of the Convention's authority was also expressed in its delegation of many *conventionnels* to special duties with particular armies or in particular departments; these were the '*représentants en mission*' and they had overriding powers which many of them used ferociously. But, of course, they had to use them within the context of possibilities provided by local forces, and if they did not agree with or subdue the local militants, it was not easy for them to proceed.

This is the basic reason why it is so difficult to say how revolutionary government worked in practice. Although the principle of centralized authority had never been abandoned and was in the end reasserted in practice, local conditions were always paramount. This was not just because local militants and the emissaries from the Convention who sought to control and cajole them faced different degrees of opposition and therefore enjoyed different degrees of success in carrying out standard policies; in many instances they were actually trying to do different things—sometimes to soothe local populations and sometimes to intimidate them, for example. Circumstance (above all, the differing attitudes of local communities) created a huge variety of responses to the major executive initiative of the revolution, the battle for survival.

Consciousness of the opposition it faced and awareness of the penalties of the costs of failure explains much of the violence of revolutionary government. Many people died:

over 100,000 rebels, it seems, in the fighting or the repression which followed. Many others suffered maltreatment, assault, the seizure of their property, imprisonment. This was not unremarked by contemporaries, nor has it been by historians, though perhaps we are now in danger of somewhat under-rating such horrors because of the callousing our imaginations have undergone under the impact of much larger-scale brutalities. Much of the impression produced on contemporaries, though, was by the warfare of words; the rhetoric of the era leant towards a violent style. Revolutionary *cliché* and habitual usage were more and more marked by forceful images and affirmations as the years went by. The supreme example, perhaps, was the semi-official adoption of the word 'Terror' which subsequently gave its name to the whole episode looked at under the rubric of 'revolutionary govern-ment'. Not that violence itself was new; it was the setting of life under the old regime. What was new was that it was now legitimized; the great outbursts of popular violence had been mythologized into epiphanies of the Revolution.

Much of the Terror was mindless. It was not an ordered movement, sweeping France irresistibly towards a clear goal of political and social reform, though some of its proponents hoped it might be and many of its enemies feared it was. If it had a pervasive principle, it was one more often implicit than explicit and it lay in the fact that what all those involved in it were trying to do—save France—required the biggest attempt yet seen to nationalize the life of a whole State, to regulate it in all its aspects from a central source of impulse and to make all Frenchmen and Frenchwomen feel the reality of nationhood.

In this, the men of the Convention were not completely successful, but they did marvellous things and achieved more than any earlier government. They thus changed the world indirectly, by raising a new standard of administrative achievement; they suggested a new possibility of what a state might do if based on national will. Apart from this, the lasting results of their efforts were, with one exception, more negative. It can hardly be doubted that the Terror hardened attitudes, for good and bad, both for and against the Revolution. A new bitterness was born of it, even if many Frenchmen felt a new commitment to the Revolution when it was over. The outstanding example was the precipitation of a Catholic anti-revolutionary sentiment which was to provide a datum of French politics for the next century. Whatever doubts existed earlier, the September Massacres opened a period in which the Revolution was regarded by most Catholics as anti-Christian.

Yet none of these effects can detract from the greatest achievement of revolutionary government, the simple fact of survival. It took France through the moment when the Revolution might have perished. It changed little, but made possible the maintenance of the changes already achieved.

The end of the Convention

Though it is tempting to dwell only on the great days of crisis and revolutionary government, they do not concern us now except for the scars they left. In any case, the Convention outlasted this heroic period and did much besides striving to manage the Terror. The decree of 14 *Frimaire* can be seen as a political as well as an institutional marker. The same men continued to lead the nation after it as before —they were increasingly identified as the associates and toadies of Robespierre, a deputy from Arras who had been a radical almost from the start of the Revolution—but they operated in a different climate. It is easier to sense the expressions of this than to say when it actually came about, but it was marked by a growing confidence on their part. For all the constitutional theorizing about the equivalence of the legal standing of committees of the Convention, in the public eye that government was the Committee of Public Safety, which appeared to be dominated by Robespierre and those who thought like him.

Argument continues both about the realism of such an assessment and about what Robespierre's true purposes were and who shared them. What remains indisputable is that under his leadership, the Convention again and again authorized measures which strengthened the Committee's grip on affairs and did so in part by further formal applications of 'Terror'—increasing the powers of the Revolutionary Tribunal, striking down centres of alleged counter-revolution even when they were found among popular leaders or within the Convention itself, passing legislation against suspects. During this period the practical organization of war-making also went on more effectively than before. The serious defects of the *Maximum* were assessed and a more complex and economically sophisticated set of price controls was authorized at the beginning of 1794.

All this represented a great practical increase in the powers and efficiency of government (though the frictional drag on turning law into practice must never be forgotten; months later, when the *Maximum* was abolished, its revised scales had not yet begun to operate in some parts of the country). It was based upon the defeat of counter-revolution at home, the assurance of supplies to the army and cheap food to Paris, and on the gradual assertion of control over the extremists who had so often caused uproar and awoken opposition. As 1794 went on, it became evident that this success had strengthened government against the left as well as against the right. As the emergency receded, less attention had to be paid to Parisian agitators (the Commune of Paris, the municipal governing body, was, in any case, firmly in the hands of Robespierre supporters from the spring onwards). The feeling that the country (and the Revolution) was saved is a part of the explanation why the *sansculotte* accepted this change; it seems inherently plausible, too, that as the months went by those who had better things to do with their time in a period of struggling business found their revolutionary energies waning. They may also have registered by their acquiescence the fact that only the exceptional and truly revolutionary personality can keep up indefinitely excitement such as that of the heady days of 1792–3.

All this adds up to saying that in the early months of 1794 France was governed as perhaps she had never been before; though this might not seem much to a modern man, used to an all-pervading State machine of considerable effectiveness, it was very striking to contemporaries. The impulse from the centre was a reality, whatever qualifications attended its operation in the periphery. But political success is rarely undiluted; in the Terror it undermined the system itself which had produced it. The persecution of one set of popular leaders after another on charges which seem to do little but mask their essential guilt (in the eyes of the Government) in providing a possible alternative leadership for the Revolution, and the increasing dominance of Parisian administration and the clubs by men dependable from the point of view of the Committee of Public Safety created weaknesses. Like the decree of 14 *Frimaire*, these developments antagonized some revolutionaries; in those who were less concerned it encouraged the growth of a mood of indifference towards the men in power which was very unlike the enthusiasm with which their acts had been sustained some months before. When, as happened during the summer, they undertook policies which were unpopular (such as a wage-freeze in Paris) or easily misunderstood (such as the legislation of a new revolutionary 'Cult of the Supreme Being' in an endeavour to cut a way through the tangle of religious issues dividing Frenchmen), the politicians at the head of affairs could not call on the popular support they had formerly enjoyed nor on the allegiance of the men who had usually been able to mobilize it.

There were effects among the politicians themselves, too, and they came to the surface violently in July 1794. Here we approach one of the uncharted areas of the Revolution, the political thinking of the Convention itself. The problem is posed by the outline of a well-known story. The Convention was elected in September 1792. For a year, its members moved slowly towards the jettisoning of inhibitions against strong measures; they succumbed to popular pressure behind the Jacobin argument that it was necessary to proceed to extremes, even in sacrificing some of the Revolution's gains, in order to preserve the Revolution. During the ascendancy of the Committee of Public Safety to which this gave rise, there was almost no opposition within the Convention to the legislation put before it and the direction it received from above. Then, by a quick reversal, it overthrew the Committee.

In a sudden confrontation, Robespierre and his friends were within a few hours removed from power, arrested and executed in the days of *Thermidor*, the month whose name was ever afterwards to be associated with this crisis. The Convention then set about dismantling the apparatus of revolutionary government and turned towards the problem of reinstating constitutional government, which it did by writing a new constitution (the Constitution of the Year III, as it is called) and pursuing its enemies to left and right even more ferociously than revolutionary government had ever done.

For a variety of reasons, we know very little about the precise movements of opinion within the Convention which made this reversal possible. As well as the 'Mountain', observers distinguished within it also a 'stomach' (*Ventre*) or a 'marsh' (*Marais*) which made up a mass of opinion waiting to be given a lead. But this takes us hardly any way. There were, too, discernible small groups of *conventionnels* earlier associated with particular politicians. But we really know very little about their precise motives.

What seems to have happened in the crisis of *Thermidor* is that former supporters were alienated from Robespierre and his friends (the Committee of Public Safety was itself divided, some of its members participating in his overthrow) and that this opposition was reinforced by more extreme revolutionaries, whose wishes had earlier been thwarted by the imposition of the committee's control. It is also clear that many *conventionnels* who had soldiered on with the regime while the crisis lasted now felt that it was asking too much of them at a moment when the emergency was dissipating. A new law reorganizing the Revolutionary tribunal had been followed by an intensification of the Terror at Paris in June and July. Some deputies were frightened by the danger of a political dictatorship based on further purging of the Convention itself, though the law was voted. Some of them, too, were offended by specific recent measures such as the new official cult, thinking that such steps proved Robespierre was a tyrant in the making. However we estimate the balance of these forces, the upshot was *Thermidor*, and the Thermidorians were successful because the forces outside the Convention which might have rallied to Robespierre and his companions had themselves been alienated.

The execution of the Robespierre clique was not quite the last demonstration that the Convention still could not change a government without bloodshed; a ferocious purge followed for a few weeks more. But then began a milder period. The dismantling of revolutionary government went steadily forward through the winter, the ascendancy of the Committee of Public Safety having almost at once been restricted. This was a key decision; *Thermidor* was the beginning of the re-assertion of parliamentary government, not the end of appeals to violence; the *conventionnels* were the real rulers of France once more. And the interests of France which they now strove to uphold were, somewhat more nakedly than they had been for a while, those of property-holders.

The Constitution of the Year III and after

It was not long before the Convention embarked on new policies. The *Maximum*, first suspended, was finally abolished on Christmas Eve 1794. Revolutionary extremists in the political clubs and sections were pursued directly and indirectly (the Jacobin Club itself was closed down) and the survivors of those deputies expelled at the time of the coup which ejected the Girondins were readmitted to the Convention. Such steps have been seen by historians of the establishment tradition which has dominated French revolutionary scholarship since the beginning of this century as a simple evolution towards the Right. There has been a consistent tendency to see a degeneration in the revolution after *Thermidor* and to express it in ideological and class terms. Two recent books in a multi-volume history of modern France express this implicitly in their titles—*La République jacobine, 10 août 1792–9 thermidor an II* is followed by *La République bourgeoise de Thermidor à Brumaire, 1794–99*. It is difficult not to feel that this makes too much turn on the fall of a few; if anyone was *bourgeois*, Jacobins were. The *conventionnels* were almost the same body of men before and after *Thermidor*; they represent a human continuity at the heart of the affairs running from 1792 to 1795, and in a measure until even later. They had the last word, and when their task was done they secured the translation of a large number of themselves to the legislative assemblies which succeeded them. *Thermidor* barely interrupted this story; it expressed its essential continuity in that it was one more removal of a group of politicians who had outlived their usefulness by another group. Their removal was rendered necessary and possible by their own success; the emergency had passed.

In the months following *Thermidor* the majority of *conventionnels* showed by their legislation what the Revolution meant to them once France no longer had her back to the wall. By and large, they steered a centre course, striking down *sansculotte* and royalist (and even some of those who had pulled down Robespierre) with equal vigour, passing fresh legislation against refractory priests who were assumed to be counter-revolutionary (the French State ceased to provide any financial support for religion whatsoever in September, though liberty of worship was formally guaranteed), but offering amnesties to rebels. All this was possible because pressure on them was relaxed. Victory in the field left France by the end of 1795 with two of her major enemies, Prussia and Spain, driven to terms, and her north-western frontier safe after her armies overran Belgium and Holland. At home, an attempted landing by the *émigrés* in Brittany with the support of the English had been defeated and it began to look as if the threat of insurrection, contained by the end of 1793, was at last dying away. Above all, Paris was no longer a danger. The last dangerous attempts to intimidate the Convention came in April and May 1795; after a moment's seeming success, these movements were easily mastered. Royalist insurrection in Paris in the following October was even more swiftly and brutally crushed.

One part of this story was the waning of the spirit of the *sansculotte* movement. Its division and demoralization had begun under revolutionary government; many of its old political leaders had been killed or purged by Robespierre's friends and *Thermidor* presented puzzles of interpretation. The call for volunteers and conscription had helped too, both by providing more reliable military forces and by taking away from Paris national guardsmen and many of the unemployed who had been ready to turn out in the great insurrections. Of those who were left, many had their loyalties torn and increasingly found their economic interests at odds with those of other revolutionaries. When, finally, the Convention took the decision no earlier Assembly had dared to take and called on the army to protect the Revolution against Paris by entering the militant sections and taking away their cannon, the story of *sansculotte* violence was over, and the history of militancy becomes a story to be followed only in the police files and lists of the politically suspect. It was thirty-five years before there was another popular rising in Paris.

The Directory

A very democratic Constitution had been drawn up and adopted in the summer of 1793 but had never been put into practice. It was regarded as a symbol of egalitarian, extremist thinking and stood no chance of resurrection by the Thermidorians; a popular insurrection in support of it merely sealed its fate. Work on yet another began in March 1795; the result was submitted to a referendum in August. It embodied a return to parliamentarianism and resurrected the old division between executive and legislative which had been set aside by the practical centralization of all power in the Convention. An elected Directory of five members was to govern under the eye of a legislature in one respect novel: it was bicameral. Beyond this, the Constitution went back to a property franchise; only three members of the Convention spoke up for universal manhood suffrage. This is interesting, but even more so, at first sight, is the general acquiescence with which this rejection of democracy seemed to be received throughout the country. France, it appeared, wanted after all to be in the hands of voters who paid taxes, and electors drawn from the ranks of the better-off. The explanation of the referendum was in fact more complicated: the poll was low, and most of the abstainers were democrats.

The Paris sections, certainly, were violently against a return to a restricted franchise.

The government of France under this constitution and the particular behaviour of the individual directors who came and went between 1795 and 1799 has traditionally and conventionally attracted much unfavourable comment. This is not hard to understand *a priori*: disappointed democrats who saw 1794 as a passage from Robespierrian light to Thermidorian darkness did not wish to see any good (or even any practical justification) in the regime to which that year opened the way, while the admirers of Bonaparte did their best to blacken the reputation of the regime he overthrew in order to justify his usurpation of power. It even helped that several of the Directors themselves did their best to run down their colleagues in self-justification. As a result, the historiographical current has always run strongly against the Directory.

The justification of this, on the other hand, is harder to accept than this explanation. Obviously, in one supremely important respect the regime failed: it did not survive. In this, of course, it was like the Constituent and the Legislative. On the other hand, even in this most crucial of political tests it did comparatively better than either. It lasted longer than they and did so by a considerable margin if we recognize—as is reasonable—that the Directory was set up peacefully by the majority of the Convention and ought properly to be considered as a continuation of that regime, which expressed its true nature once rid of the worst pressures of the national emergency.

Nor is it certain that the Directory was such a practical and administrative failure as has often been said. We are only just beginning to penetrate in detail the actual workings of its government, but by combining harshness and a recognition of local realities it suffered no recommencement of the civil war. If it ignored religion officially, liberty of worship was written into its Declaration of Rights and Duties, and priests who had emigrated began to return. It stabilized financial policy after a disastrous collapse of the *assignat* and refounded the currency. It chose generals who commanded its armies in the field successfully and it conducted a skilful foreign policy within the limited area of freedom it possessed.

This area, though, was increasingly narrowed by the growing dependence of the Directory on its generals. Even in 1796, the young Bonaparte showed in Italy that a general could disobey orders if he won battles. Nor did the soldiers' power grow only because no government in Paris could easily appear to disavow victory. It also mattered that the armies were increasingly stationed abroad at the expense of other countries and the prospect of bringing them home was unwelcome for financial reasons; they provided, too, loot which took burdens off the French tax-payer; the Directory itself fell back on the army's support as its relations with the representative Councils deteriorated, and relied on it to carry out a purge of their membership in September 1797; finally, with the mastering of popular insurrection, no counterbalancing force existed inside France with which the civilian government could resist the soldiers should they decide to act in an independent political role.

It says something important for the quality of the Republic's military discipline that this did not happen overtly until 1799 and that the soldiers then acted only when an opening was provided by politicians. Civilians appealed to the soldier Bonaparte for help and gave him his opportunity, though they had wished to return to what they believed was the true constitutionalism of the Directory's early days. After growing signs of strains, the political machinery showed once again that it could not manage an agreed transfer of power. Yet the *coup d'état* of the month of *Brumaire* was not a very violent or bloody affair. The acquiescence of most Frenchmen in it and the subsequent modification of the Consulate which gave Bonaparte undisguised supremacy perhaps indicates only that the ideas and men of the Directory had outlived their time, not that they had always been wrong.

Retrospect

In assessing the discontinuities brought by the Revolution, the easiest to tick off are institutional. Laws are definite and dated, even if uncertainty surrounds their enforcement and effectiveness; they either remain on the statute-book or they do not. Less formally-defined and (sometimes) less conscious changes are harder to assess. One of the most obvious, but most intangible of those brought by the Revolution, the introduction to France, Europe, and, in the end, the whole world, of a new kind of politics, was of this sort, obvious in the long run, but difficult to pin down. It was not merely a matter of what was indicated by the terminology of the Revolution— the 'men of *Thermidor*', '*sansculottes*', the '*tutoyer*', and so on; these are of great importance in providing mental categories for the organization of the Revolution's thought about itself, but remain only symptoms of a new political world. There are deeper changes to measure, such as the actual introduction for the first time of national politics to France. The politicization of the French people in the Revolution provided the subsoil for the politics of the next century and a half and came about by many channels. One was elections; from the excitement over those to the Estates-General onward, whatever the restrictions at different times on the legal or actual size of the electorate, Frenchmen were repeatedly offered electoral choices not only for the members of Legislative, Convention, and their successors, nor only in the constitutional referenda, but in local affairs and even, for a while and in some places, for offices in the Church.

These elections took place while Frenchmen were also being politicized in other ways. The press began this even before the election of the Estates-General, by debating the form they should take and giving advice about what the *cahiers* should contain. Whatever was filtered out in their successive stages of refinement, too, the drawing-up of the *cahiers* must have been politically educative, forging for many Frenchmen the first crude links between personal resentments and grievances and the national idea, providing them with some sense of strategic priorities and a hierarchy of political purposes. Another factor was the evolution of political clubs; outside Paris their membership was often restricted, but they turned the interest of local élites hitherto unpoliticized towards specifically political issues; sometimes the membership of a masonic lodge or a reading-society became almost overnight the nucleus of a Jacobin club. The National Guard, like the short-lived urban militias from which it emerged, was another political educator; so were the sectional meetings of 1793. There was administrative participation, too; the Revolution brought a great influx of new men into local government who elbowed aside many of the *officiers* of the old regime. There was official propaganda, employed more consciously than in earlier times and, whether successful or not, sharpening the sense of the political. And finally, there was religion, which presented Frenchmen all over France with the need to argue the Revolution in a personal and concrete form: which priest, juror or non-juror?, and, later, why any priest at all?

The growing sense of emergency was a continuing stimulus to this politicization. The threat of civil war (and its reality in many places), the fear of what might follow a successful foreign invasion, the opportunities provided for rhetorical justification of policy by the legislation of revolutionary government all drove home political lessons. From a growing willingness to think in political terms at all (as opposed to thinking in the legal, moral, and religious terms of the old order) came the conceptual world of modern politics. At its heart lay the need to control the State's power, because the Revolution provided a quite new notion of what might be the possible, reasonable, and moral limits of State action. As 1815 was to show, in the end there were not enough Frenchmen who wanted to put the clock back and return to the old order to make the real 'restoration' possible on the basis of indefeasible particular privilege. Most accepted, instead, that the sovereign nation should decide how State power should be used; constitutional structures could be argued about, but their aim should be to give expression to the national will, as even Bonaparte agreed. This was to mean that most of the great political arguments of nineteenth-century France were about the nature and form of representative machinery and what list of rights should be regarded as immune to interference by the constituted powers.

A new politics implied new political institutions. Parties, eventually, were to be central ones, but during the Revolutionary decade the idea of party could not be cleared of the taint of faction. Instead, party had an underground, unofficial life, barely expressed in institutional forms which had advanced beyond those of *salon* or political club. The latter was the most important new institution in the struggle for the levers of politics, the channel for the organization of petition and mass demonstration.

Paradoxically, one reason why the idea of party was tainted was to be found in the new politics themselves. The new ideological world they announced took it for granted that social and political questions were susceptible of only one right answer. Both opponents and advocates of the Revolution espoused a political manicheism, a belief in black-and-white confrontations rather than groupings for acceptable compromise, which fed the rhetoric and imagery of the Revolution. Such an outcome should not surprise us. Centuries of Christianity lay behind the predisposition to moral absolutism; the *philosophes* had merely secularized some of its expressions. The Revolution threatened so many and such crucial personal interests that it was natural to try to force the issues into a Procrustean framework which could reduce them all to the crude vision of conflicts between liberating progress and superstitious despotism, or between dictatorial folly and pride on the one hand, and the complex and hallowed wisdom of ages of experience on the other. This false but necessary antithesis was to pass into European political life in the myth of a politics reducible to a single scale of values, the myth of Left and Right.

This way of looking at politics emerged almost accidentally from a choice of seats by like-minded men in the early days of the Constituent; observers first identified the *droite* (right), those aristocratic deputies who had taken their place in the benches on the right of the president of the assembly, and *gauche* (left) came into use later and consequentially. Thus, from a handful of personal decisions, was born the division of Right and Left which was to dominate European politics for the next century and a half. Immediately, it helped to clarify other distinctions between the legislators of 1789. From the polarization of Right and Left emerged a 'spectrum' view of politics which implied that every difference and *nuance* of political attitude could be arranged as a continuing series; soon, moderate revolutionaries and men who spoke of the Revolution being 'over' could be distinguished on this spectrum from radicals and democrats who wanted its changes to go much further. Gradually, there was to evolve in the next quarter of a century a set of terms—conservative, liberal, radical—which reflected the main distinctions within the general antithesis and took for granted an ideological spectrum wholly comprehended between these two poles.

Such terms were part of a whole collection of neologisms, adaptations of existing meanings and expressions of new moods which added up to the new vocabulary that a new sort of politics required. Some of its components went back well before 1789. A 'patriot' of that year was not merely a Frenchman whose bosom swelled with proper pride as he contemplated the achievements of his nation, but one whose inclination was towards reform, who distrusted the inheritance of despotism and identified himself with the revolutionary cause in a broad sense; some of this had already been apparent in the way the word was used in the 1770s. *Aristocrate*, *aristocratique*, *démocratie*, and *démocratique* were other words bandied about well before the Estates-General met, though their widespread use became common only in the second half of 1789. Two other old words with even greater futures ahead, 'Liberty' and 'Equality', became more common at the same time; 'Fraternity' was only to join them later and never acquired their popularity, though the combination of these three words into a slogan, which the following century took to be the most concise embodiment of the ideals of the Revolution, was achieved by 1791. Much more linguistic innovation was to follow; *sansculotte*, 'terrorist', 'Jacobin', all became highly evocative terms of political art, and 'people', 'republic', 'nation', *patrie* acquired new senses. The evolution of such words is a part of the history of other languages as well as of French. Finally, the supreme linguistic innovation was the broadening of the word 'Revolution' itself.

The expression of the new politics in words explains some of the importance attached to language by France's Jacobin rulers. As one of them put it, language had become the business of the State (*une affaire d'état*). This was in part because of the need to create a sense of nationality among communities still speaking local dialects and *patois*. It was in part a matter of assuring the communication of the governments' wishes and policies to the people through print. But the linguistic significance of the Revolution goes further than this. Ideological discontinuity reflected in a new political language was one of the greatest breaks with the past achieved in the Revolution, because it went down deep into the minds of men. It broadened, narrowed, and delimited afresh the ways men could see and understand what was happening to them. This was one of many ways in which 1789 opened a new era in mentality, sensibility, and civilization, as well as in politics.

4

The Revolution as continuity

THE most casual visitor quickly discovers that for all the strenuous and self-conscious innovation of her recent rulers, France remains a deeply conservative country. Her conservatism is rooted in the Revolution itself: it was then that much took shape and hardened which was to prove so enduring. So we confront a paradox: from this great upheaval, with all its novelty and liberating force, stemmed a huge inertia.

The paradox deepens when we look more closely, for the Revolution was not just a matter of initiating a new era, installing new vested interests and then going over on to a conservative tack. The more closely they are studied, the more striking are the continuities which stretch across 1789. The Revolution preserved, and even revivified, much of the past. Contemporary interpreters did not miss the continuities, though they saw them in different ways. Condorcet spoke for many educated men in sensing the culmination of a movement of liberation stretching back across the centuries; some such interpretation was implicit in most progressive and 'enlightened' views and came out in the iconography and rhetoric of revolution which installed busts of Rousseau and celebrated feasts of Reason in former cathedrals, and acclaimed tyrannicide by rescuing Brutus from eighteen centuries of historical condemnation. What is more, opponents of the Revolution agreed that it was a climax in a long maturing development. Now-forgotten writers found ready acceptance for their views that the roots of the wickedness of their day were to be sought in the great assertion of human pride they saw in the Protestant Reformation.

Such claims of ideological continuity now seem uncon-
vincing (though not to be dismissed out of hand: we shall
need to look at them again), but the line of 1789 (or 1792,
or 1794, or any other date) was also to be increasingly blurred
by scholarship. Continuity with the old order *(ancien régime)*,
is the central theme of what is arguably the greatest book
on the Revolution (that by Tocqueville); since it appeared
over a century ago, a huge literature has set out more facts
which suggest and sometimes explicitly argue that the Revolution marked no such cataclysmic discontinuity in French
history as its violent moments and political mythology might
suggest. We should beware of exaggerating events, however
dramatic, and reflect that for all the bloody upheavals much
of France and many Frenchmen witnessed in the 1790s, their
impact, though sometimes terrible in personal terms, can have
been little different in kind from what was undergone by areas
troubled by peasant revolt and royal punitive measures in
the seventeenth century, for example, and was in some cases
far less severe. About such episodes, appalling as they could
be, we do not use the word 'revolution'.

The long run

In reflecting on such matters, some people have gone so far
as to say that in many ways the Revolution only provided
new forms and channels for forces at work long before it broke
out, to whose effect it made little difference. Such an approach
is somewhat encouraged if we look at some of those fundamental trends in social and economical life which can only
be observed in the long run—what French historians have
called *la longue durée*. Population history is an instance. One
change is indisputable: whereas eighteenth-century France
was a country where a growing population pressed steadily
and heavily on resources (and this, indeed, was intrinsic
to the crisis of the Revolution itself), Frenchmen became more
and more obsessed as the nineteenth century wore on with
the fears and problems of under-population. In the long run
of a century or so, that is to say, French demography
underwent a radical transformation and wherever we begin

or end it, the Revolution falls inside that period. How it is related to this prolonged change is very hard to say, though.

Once we focus upon the Revolutionary decade itself, even many of the facts are still in doubt. Much poorer statistical information about French demography is available between 1785 and 1806 than for the years before or after. The last ministers of the old monarchy showed less interest in gathering data than their recent predecessors had done. Into this relaxed situation broke the administrative upheavals of the Revolution. For much of 1789–90 France was virtually ungoverned in so far as the detailed application of administrative processes were concerned: even tax-gathering broke down in some areas, a crucial test. Then came Revolutionary Government; it reasserted the grip of government but had more urgent tasks than collecting population data. When this was resumed, it was in a new world, administratively speaking. The new framework of Departments and Communes had replaced the old provinces, generalities, and immunities. Furthermore, there were annexed territories not belonging to France in 1789. As for system, the local administrative authorities had taken over responsibility for the *état civil*—the recording of births, marriages, and deaths—which had once belonged to the parish priest. All this means that comparison with what had gone before would be very difficult even had the records been continuously and accurately kept. But invasion, civil war, and a running social indiscipline played havoc with the reliability of such as survived. After the worst crisis, when things settled down again somewhat under the Directory, it is difficult to avoid the conclusion that this was at least in part because that regime tacitly accepted that much of France could not be governed in the teeth of the opposition of many Frenchmen; in so far as this concerns us here, this means that the administered rather than the administrators determined what got into the records and what did not.

One conclusion which seems probable is that there was substantial under-recording of births throughout the later 1790s. Under the Consulate, when the new 'Prefects' appointed to administer Departments were asked for population information, their reports themselves drew attention to the inadequacy of the administrative procedures on which they had to rest; however firm their beliefs about what was happening, they were unable to substantiate them with facts. There is the continuing problem of war, too. From 1792 to 1814 (with only one short interval), France was continuously at war with at least one other major power and the estimation of the cost in casualties and its demographic effect involves yet another set of unknowns in her population history.

Notwithstanding these hindrances, French historians have done their best in recent years to make some headway with such material as they have. The results may be regarded as tentative, but all point towards an overall continuity with the patterns of the *ancien régime* which persists well after 1800. This hypothesis makes sense of well-known facts about the nineteenth-century French economy: the French continued to suffer recurrent dearths right down to the 1840s, so that in the Revolution population growth did not lose its old tendency to outrun production. Moreover, the Napoleonic statistics suggest a rise in population of nearly two millions between 1790 and 1806; refining this, the latest estimates suggest that about 1.3 millions of this figure may be allocated to the 1790s themselves. This is what we might expect; the removal of some legal and social restraints, together with conscription and the opportunities presented by turbulent times encouraged more people to marry or to run the risk of children born out of wedlock and to this extent the Revolution reinforced the trend of a rising population visible under the *ancien régime*. Whatever weight we give to such speculation though, the one conclusion which *cannot* be squared with our evidence is that France made a break with her demographic past in the 1790s. The knowledge of contraception, evidence of which before 1789 has so excited demographic historians, may have continued to spread, and the slow pressures which made smaller families seem more attractive may have already begun to operate in the 1790s, but neither produced any speedy or striking rupture with the past. Short-term fluctuations, such as the steep rise in marriages in 1793–4 (which it is hard to attribute to anything but the exemption of married men from conscription) and a consequent peak in the registration of births soon after can be detected, but over the whole decade, after all allowances are made for the inadequacy of the data, the safest judgement seems to be that French population history did not enter a phase distinguishable from that of the *ancien régime*.

It would, of course, be rather surprising if it had done. Population history above all is history *à la longue durée* and the working through of the innovations in economic possibility and mentality which are the motors of demographic change can hardly be expected to be apparent within a decade, except in highly developed societies. This does not mean that the 1790s did not inaugurate and release forces ultimately leading to such changes, only that their operation would be no more visible to a Frenchman (or a Frenchwoman) in 1799 than they had been ten years earlier: life would be as hard (or easy) and the size of a family and the likelihood of its members surviving infancy hardly different at those two dates. The big changes were to come later, when a decisive break was made in the early nineteenth century—we still do not know exactly how—with older ways. It was then that the prolific France of the eighteenth century, with its appalling hunger, pitiful crops of foundlings and hordes of beggars gave way to the France of cautiously limited family size, virtually self-sufficient in food, losing steadily the military superiority that sheer numbers had given the armies of Louis XIV and Napoleon.

The economy

So intimately linked are demographic and economic questions that this is the obvious place to consider continuities in the economy (or the lack of them). At the outset, we might remark that the question is badly put; only an economist can find it useful—and he only for limited purposes—to speak of *the* French economy in the eighteenth century. France was a country of local markets, local prices, dependent on local supply and demand; more general factors were hardly beginning to pull these into some sort of unity before 1789. The most common shared experience was that of dearth; nature was still the major economic determinant. Even the potentially standardizing effect of government policy, acutely aware as it was of the primacy of considerations of public order, was filtered through many local and particular exemptions and privileges so that the assumption of regulation entailed no assumption of regularity; the outstanding example was the division between provinces paying heavy taxes on salt and the rest, a division which effectively created specialized local economies based on smuggling, and special opportunities of employment for children and women in border districts. One of the major changes of the Revolution was the removal of the extra layer of fragmentation provided by such arrangements.

One reason for the predominance of local markets and local economies was the lack of big cities. Most Frenchmen lived in communities of less than 10,000 people and of this group the vast majority were peasants. Paris in 1789 was the greatest city of France and had about a half-million inhabitants; Lyons came a long way behind with about a quarter of that number, and was rivalled only by Bordeaux with 110,000 or so. The other provincial cities of France might be important bishoprics, sites of fortresses, old markets, but they were for the most part small places (only 38 towns had more than 30,000 people). Only one category of towns had shown really vigorous growth in the eighteenth century, the major ports, among which Bordeaux (which had more than doubled its population) was outstanding.

This was because such towns were engaged in the only economic activity in eighteenth-century France which showed spectacular growth and improvement: overseas trade. With the Levant through Marseilles, above all with the Americas through Nantes and Bordeaux, it had shot up. In particular, while trade with other European countries quintupled, that with the colonies multiplied tenfold. Yet the pace was already slackening in the 1780s. Nor did the general commercial activity of which this was the most thriving part compare with England's. French financial and commercial institutions were rudimentary. There were some big wholesalers and important financiers (*capitalistes*, as they were called) who could mobilize funds to lend to the State, but banking was rudimentary and the absence of a true national market confined such men to local activity for the most part. International bankers lived in Holland or Switzerland.

Nonetheless, the overall growth of commerce during the century was appreciable and encouraging. Industry was more backward. Large enterprises were unusual; small-scale artisan production and the putting-out of materials to cottage workers were the characteristic forms of production. A few privileged monopolies and joint-stock enterprises provided the only large works.

Against this background, it is understandable that land was everywhere the preferred destination of savings: this much at least is an acceptable generalization about the eighteenth-century French economy. Often this was agricultural land. Agriculture was the backbone of the economy. Although France could not be certain of its self-sufficiency, agriculture was in the first place important because on it depended the actual survival of the people; this was where their food came from in normal times. Secondly, it was the largest employer, directly and indirectly. Thirdly, it was the main absorbent of investment.

For all the luxuriant variety of methods, tenures, economic relationships, and social reality which makes up the world of the French country-dweller under the old order, the agricultural sector as a whole dominated the economy. Yet however manful the efforts of some individuals and however prosperous some areas, French farming was backward and inefficient except in the minimal sense that it had fed (with help from abroad) a growing population, albeit at a lower standard in the 1780s than earlier in the century. And the problem of recurrent famine still existed, as the events of 1788 and 1789 themselves showed. Though a normal harvest was enough to keep starvation at bay, productivity had not grown at a rate which kept pace with the growth of population and the result was continuing price inflation and falling standards of living. Such facts suggest that the agricultural effect of the Revolution was small: as has already been pointed out, dearth did not cease magically in 1789—or ten years later, or twenty-five for that matter. Yet this is not the whole story; we have to look a little closer to assess the impact of the Revolution and its limits. Obviously, the local, personal, and immediate effect of the abolition of the 'feudal system' or of the sale of a large ecclesiastical estate could be very great indeed. The effect of such changes on the overall output and efficiency of French agriculture is much harder to establish and, whatever its extent, is only to be observed after years or decades have passed.

The impact of policy

This provides a clue towards assessing changes in economic life brought by the Revolution. If these are looked at in the short perspective, then many important acts of policy must be recorded. Under the Constituent Assembly, they were dominated by economic liberalism; it was a period of legis-lative innovation, even if the rulers of France did not go the whole hog and abandon protectionism and privilege for the colonial trade. Nonetheless, the breaking-down of professional restrictionism and the passing of laws against corporations show a new decisiveness in legislation. So (once the crisis of 1789 was past) did the determined preservation by the Con-stituent of internal free trade in grain and the abolition of other restraints (such as internal customs areas and fiscal distinctions between localities) which provided a legal carapace for the internal markets of old France. Good harvests and the maintenance of external commerce until the coming of the war favoured it. 1790–2 were years of economic well-being by comparison with what had gone before; it may not be too much to speak of a boom.

Yet this does not take us far in assessing the specific impact of the Revolution *per se*, for, once more, a long-term perspec-tive may affect judgements. In many ways, the Constituent was only putting into practice what had been tried in-effectually by many ministers under the old order. It was Turgot who in 1775 first abolished the *jurandes*, the guilds which controlled Parisian trades, thus anticipating Le Chapelier's anti-combination law. Turgot had also introduced an important measure of free trade in grain (thus provoking widespread rioting and disorder). Later ministers tried the same tack; it was up-to-the-minute economic thinking in the 1770s and 1780s to suggest that the right course for economic management was not mercantilism but *laissez-faire*. The weakening of external protection, too, had begun in 1786, with the commercial treaty with England which was almost at once blamed for the depression soon settling on the northern manufacturing areas.

The next phase of the Revolution brought a swing back to interference with the economy. Here, too, there was continuity rather than rupture with the past, as is evident from what has just been said, though this time it is continuity in response to the conservative demands of the French consumer. The *conventionnels* were forced into acceptance of a new *dirigisme* by insurrection, riot, the seizure of foodstuffs on the road, and forced auctions and sales at acceptable prices (*taxation populaire*) like those which had confronted Turgot's officials in 1775. The dominating factor in the background was, of course, different, for it was the war—and this was clearly attributable to the Revolution. Yet the war drove the Revolution off course, economically speaking, in order to achieve the mobilization necessary for victory. Levies in kind replaced taxation in many places—a clear sign of retrogression in the fiscal system from the improved rationality and equity which the Constituent had intended. As inflation made it more and more attractive to hold goods and the elasticity ebbed out of commerce, demands arose for more savage laws against hoarding or the holding-back of supplies in anticipation of a favourable price. The central innovation was the *Maximum*, but this was an innovation in manner rather than in principle. Instead of the assurance of supplies to local markets being the responsibility of the *intendant*, who under the old order normally proceeded to use his powers to maintain local custom and practice, the new price-fixing was envisaged as a national matter. The *Maximum* was in this respect one of the first expressions of the wish to manage a national economy such as the war required. Its enforcement was to be assured by Terror, moreover.

After *Thermidor*, France entered a phase of renewed economic liberalism. Many controls disappeared; deflation was sought through currency reform. Yet the exigencies and chances of war (now going more favourably for France) continued to require interference with economic life. Such interference increasingly reverted to the old mercantilist and protectionist forms familiar in pre-Revolutionary days. War in the end came to count for more than interests or ideology in determining the shape of economic legislation, and did more to accelerate the move towards a nationalization of economic life (though this took place, of course, on ground cleared by the institutional reforms of the Constituent). But the war also finished off the expansion of overseas trade; by 1805 Bordeaux had less than 100,000 inhabitants again. Moreover, when seeking to understand the sluggishness of French economic growth, it must be remembered that the loss of the West Indies and the blockade severely restricted French access to raw materials still available to British manufacturers.

Government became a great purchaser and consumer and its pervasiveness gave economic life a somewhat less localized structure, but however enhanced its powers seemed when compared with those visible elsewhere, it could not do very much. Probably its indirect influence through purchasing had as much effect on the structural development of the economy as anything it tried to accomplish through conscious policy. Innovations in agricultural practice sponsored by government had no more impact on the ideas of peasant-exploiters than had the ideas of the agricultural societies of the old order. True, the forms adopted for the sales of national lands did result, broadly, in the successful distribution of this property in a way which favoured the 'wager on the strong' implicit in economic liberalization, but there did not follow a sudden burst of agricultural improvement and advance such as would have set France on a course of rural change like that which England was undergoing. Instead, the flow of new property into the hands of those who were already landlords or tenants tended to confirm the general economic patterns of each region and locality and to ensure the continuing dominance of established notions of cultivation and management. As before, only more so, was the broad effect.

As for the industrial sector, where there was no such structural shift as was embodied in the confiscation of Church lands to provide a major push, the same verdict holds with perhaps even greater force. Such changes as there were grew out of the war and new demands for specialized products, or out of the use of French victory—notably during the Empire—to rig up a European protectionist system which helped France's manufacturers at the expense of her allies and satellites. Of technological innovation there was little; war and blockade may even have slowed what there was by ending such competitive innovation as that stimulated in textiles by the 1786 treaty and the subsequent introduction of 'English machines' much denounced in the *cahiers* of 1789. Nor did concentration make much progress; some was visible in cloth-making by about 1810, but in no sense did this match the advance towards factory manufacture in England.

To sense how easy it is to exaggerate the Revolution's impact on the bedrock of the French economy, it is best to take a very long step into the future and to look at it in the middle of the nineteenth century. By then, certainly, something much more like a true national market was in being; in this sense, many consequences of the breakup of the old order had worked through to practical effect, though other tendencies—the appearance of the first railways and the improvement of road and water communication in the early nineteenth century must be reckoned among them—are difficult to separate in their effects. Beyond this, though, the general impression is still one of an economy developing only slowly towards the world of rapidly increasing wealth envisaged by eighteenth-century *laissez-faire* economists and postulated by Marxist analysts of the Revolution as the triumph of the French *bourgeoisie*.

The country landscape of the mid-nineteenth century would have still been sadly comprehensible to the agronome of 1789; one scholar claimed that medieval agriculture was still going on in the part of Normandy he examined in 1850. French farming technique remained lamentably backward;

the scythe had not by then replaced the sickle, and the survival of small units of exploitation helped to keep production generally low in relation to area and labour employed. Some landlords strove to innovate and succeeded (perhaps the one unequivocal benefit conferred upon his country by Lafayette, the master of the palace of 1789, was his introduction of Merino sheep to the Orléanais in the 1820s): all exploiters of land no doubt benefited from the removal of obstacles to the release of individualism by the Constituent, but those who used this freedom to innovate and improve remained a minority just because effective control of exploitation in France was in the hands of millions of peasants. This was as conservative in its effect as before 1789, though the rural France of those days had suffered the additional encumbrance of the seigneurial system. Grimmer evidence still of the slow advance of agricultural improvement in France was to be found in the recurrence well into the nineteenth century of periods of dearth and near-famine; the eventual alleviation of this scourge was as much a matter of better arrangements for importing grain as of growing productivity.

Nor was industrial France transformed out of recognition by the middle of the seventeenth century, though its appearance had changed rather more visibly since 1789 than had that of farming. It was still dominated by artisan production in the 1840s, still relying much on putting-out. Though attitudes were changing, land or houses remained under the July Monarchy the most favoured destination for savings; though increasingly buttressed by interest from stocks and shares, property was still the main source of income other than wages. As much as she was a nation of peasant-farmers, France was a nation of proprietor-investors.

An expansion of the commercial sector had been more noteworthy and this is a part of the story of the continuing growth of the towns. Again, though, the impression overall is of gradual rather than dramatic change, and it is certainly not change easily and directly attributable to the Revolution alone. When, in 1806, the Napoleonic administration set about the compilation of adequate population statistics once more, less than one Frenchman in ten lived in towns of more than 10,000 people; Paris, Marseilles, and Lyons were by then the only three cities of more than 100,000 (there had been four in 1789) and there were only 6 of more than 50,000.

Evidently, the Revolution did not suddenly transform the fragmented, low-level economic life of eighteenth-century France into an integrated *bourgeois*-capitalist economy, though it accelerated movement in this direction. Even this contribution to change, though, was rooted in projects and ideas —and even in governmental policies—adumbrated and sometimes initiated before 1789. It is therefore hard to apply the neat logic of cause and effect to the Revolution's economic impact. The reason is that the Revolution was itself part of a much larger process, the swing throughout the European world towards market society, the change from status to contract with all the complicated cultural and mental adjustments which that implied. That some of the most important institutional changes of the Revolution made easier the change to such a society is certain; but not much more than this, that is both generally true and more specific, can be said about its economic outcome.

People

Does this amount to saying that life was therefore not very different for most people? In some important ways, it does; those who lived through the Revolution expected to die at about the same age as their fathers, have about as many children survive as did their mothers, work with tools not much different from those they had learnt to use with their first masters, and till fields that looked much the same. Were they marginally worse-off or better-off in real terms? Here the picture begins to fragment again; the weight of feudal dues had gone from the peasant, but this benefited the proprietor, lease-holder, or share-cropper rather than hired hands. Where (as in eastern France, for example) feudalism had been an especially heavy burden before 1789, the betterment was probably more obvious than elsewhere. Other burdens had changed their nature, too; the tax system was rationalized and made more equitable by the Revolution, but (as is always true in undeveloped rural economies) still oppressed the poorest because it is very difficult to prevent an undue proportion of the burden coming to rest in the end on their shoulders. Service in the royal militia had gone, but there was conscription instead.

This may reasonably lead us to the conclusion that almost every general question about the Revolutionary years is hard to answer, but none is harder than one about their effects on individuals. A vague pattern is easy enough to see: the Revolution had no direct and obvious effects on a large number of people, had indirect effects of varying degrees of importance on virtually everyone, and brought catastrophic upheavals to the lives of some. But so general an answer is unsatisfying. To categorize more precisely, though, even within well-defined groups, is much harder.

For most people, life is the business of getting a living; we might begin there and it takes us back to the economic fluctuations familiar under the old monarchy which did not stop with the Revolution. The Revolution brought big new economic opportunities, though, in the boom of the years down to 1792, and the war added to them. Some benefited throughout; perhaps most Frenchmen did between 1790 and 1792. The other side of the coin was the dislocation of supply which followed when producers and consumers tried to anticipate shortages, or which derived from the actual shortages caused by the war's demands and the shifts in requirements for labour. When the royal Court closed down aristocratic spending dried up, and when building dropped off because of uncertainty, unemployment was bound to follow. All these things affected millions of people. And, of course, inflation affected almost everybody.

Yet just this example brings us back to the difficulty of generalizing. Inflation struck very differently at the Parisian family faced by prices which threatened it with starvation, and the yeoman-farmer (*laboureur*) who could find a way of hanging on to his grain. Rising prices mattered less to those Parisian families whose breadwinners were in regular skilled employment in 1793 than to the poor who relied on casual labouring for earnings; different groups suffered at different moments of the inflationary cycle. Political and governmental conditions mattered, too—there was a lot of difference between *laboureurs* (to return to that untypical minority) in the Paris region, threatened by domiciliary searches for stored grain, and *laboureurs* who sat on their local revolutionary committees, ruling the roost in, say, the Puy-de-Dôme, and using their power to enforce wage-controls, but not controls on prices.

This may suggest that our only hope of assessing the impact of the Revolution on individuals is to proceed by looking at small groups, and perhaps localities, one by one, and thus compiling a mosaic of information which would reveal a pattern. To do that would go far beyond the scope of this little book, but even if it were contemplated, there would be point in reflecting that though the Revolution may not have had the same impact upon all Frenchmen and Frenchwomen, at least in one respect it opened up their lives in a quite new way, because of its individualism and legal egalitarianism. Careers were—as a famous phrase put it—to be open to talent. It remained to be seen what talents would prove most appropriate in the world provided by the ending of guilds, the abolition of primogeniture, the standardization of weights and measures, the ending of mortmain (to take but a few examples), but however it might work out in practice, France in the Revolution had made a great stride from status to contract. When marriage became merely a civil matter and not a sacramental tie, many new possibilities existed for the lives of individuals, even if habit and the pressure of social approval long concealed this in many parts of France.

Some of these changes were to have a standardizing effect, but did so only very slowly. It was a very long time before even the visible, let alone the mental, distinctions of province and locality which separated Frenchmen from one another were worn away. Yet the Revolution began the imposition of the national language in many parts of France and it is hard to believe that this did not mean new possibilities and perhaps changes of outlook for many individuals. For men, conscription was another nationalizing force, and so, though strongly so for only a minority, was the collective excitement of the Revolution itself, its rhetoric, festivals, and mythology.

Unfortunately, such effects tend to be most visible only in the lives of untypical men. The Louis-Clovis Berthier who in the Year II changes his first names ('because they smacked of tyranny') to Epictetus sounds as if he was an individualist from the start, but though many people took the chance to rebaptise themselves with impeccably republican names, most did not. The William Tells, Brutuses, Valerius-Publicolas, and Helvétiuses, and even those who fell back on such mild transformations as Amitié, were only a minority. Yet to such people the Revolution could bring the overturning of their lives. Years of personal frustration were suddenly cast aside by some, long-concealed but cherished hatreds were indulged, old scores long settled were reopened by men who found themselves members of local watch committees, agents or commissaries of the national government and, indeed, members of the national assembly itself. Without the Revolution, Mirabeau would be remembered only as a clever and dissolute nobleman and Robespierre at best as an ornament of the Arras bar. As a contemporary remarked, pinning down one characteristic of the Revolution in a phrase, it was 'everybody's revenge' (*la revanche de tout le monde*)—for lifetimes of unrecorded slights, wounds, and imagined grievances.

Such instances, though, cannot sustain much generalization. In some parts of the South, for example, we find that the Revolution simply provided new freedom, forms, and occasions for the expression of old hatreds between Protestant and Catholic; it did not create them, but the Revolution had a very special flavour in those areas because they were there. We are back with the difficulty of generalizing: it is hard to say that much difference—or even that an important difference—was made to men's lives when they would have quarrelled anyway, Revolution or not. Perhaps there is no line to be drawn here, only a need to bear in mind the fact that Revolution undoubtedly made violence easier over much of France. If you were a Protestant Jacobin lynched by Catholic peasants then a very important difference had been made to you by the Revolution; it would not impress the surviving relatives that the only difference from pre-

Revolutionary times was that the lynchers had then lacked opportunity and excuse. Any crumbling of the habitual restraints on violence, provision of new possibilities of self-justification, or practical upheaval in the administrative and police apparatus was bound to release violence remarkable even in a violent age. It produced a great increase in the sheer unpredictability and adventurousness of life. Of such conditions were born crime, political purges, and *coups*, and the accidents which left men staring at the power which lay at their feet or in the gutter—until they thought to pick it up.

Such unpredictable occasions and opportunities were probably more frequent in towns than in the countryside. But even in rural France, individuals might feel great changes: after all, some men were still serfs at the beginning of August 1789. Presumably they became wage-earners and there may not have been much observable difference in their daily lives as a result, but we must be careful not to rush to judgements about even so precisely defined a group. As for the overall condition of the peasantry, the only safe conclusion appears to be that unless he was very poor, the sort of peasant who drew all his income from working land had to be very unlucky —or very careless—to be actually worse off. If he had access to capital in the form of land, then he was likely to profit in proportion to his wealth, for the general tendency of the Revolution in the countryside was to remove restraints and charges on the use of the land. Insofar as land changed hands, too (and a great deal did), all the signs point to the biggest acquisition of new property being made by those who already had some (which is what might be expected *a priori*). Not only were attempts to favour the poorer would-be purchaser long ineffective, but when the law did come round to favouring him, most of the Church lands had been sold. The position of the poorest of all probably worsened, too, in other ways. They had benefited from their exploitation of communal rights of collecting wood, pasturing stock, cutting turf, and running pigs on commons—all of them legal rights which disappeared in the Revolution, along with other relics of 'feudalism'.

It is almost as hard to generalize about noblemen (let alone noblewomen) as about peasants. At first sight, the problem is simple; legal nobility is a clearly defined category, and the Revolution brought many legal changes which affected those it denoted. Primogeniture—which made possible the maintenance of estates intact—tax privileges and noble status itself were abolished. Beyond this lay a less easily defined mass of real advantages and privileges which noblemen enjoyed because they were noble. But even there, distinctions creep in; not all nobles had equal access to such advantages and many of them were shared with non-nobles. With the abolition of the *parlements* went something more tangible, an important ability to influence the public life of France in the direction of the values and assumptions of the nobility, but this change was not only of concern to the legal nobility. Finally, of course, there was the brute fact of social defeat; even if followed by later revival and recovery, the prestige (and therefore the unchallenged influence of the nobility) could never again be what it had been in 1789.

Beyond this somewhat obvious point it is hard to go. The crucial facts about economic and monetary loss—or gain—provide widely different examples; what we have is a scatter of general impressions which suggest caution. Though, for example, some big landowners suffered badly from confiscation of their property when they emigrated, other families made use of artificial transactions or other subterfuges to blunt this danger (whose impact depended in any case on the vagaries of local circumstance). But losses were not completely compensated by the indemnity provided by the French government of 1825 to former *émigrés*.

In any case, the story of the noble is not the story of the socially dominant class. It does not tell us about, for example, the non-noble rich. Some of these had *châteaux* burned early in the Revolution; some were *seigneurs* who soon found it was uphill work collecting redemption charges for their dues and had to give up. Like some noblemen; they suffered. But this does not tell us what happened to property-owners as a whole. Many, perhaps most, benefited. Noble and non-noble alike, they bought more land and urban property in the Revolution. Real estate was the best and most secure investment for professional or commercial profits and most Frenchmen with money saved tried to buy when the Revolution gave them the chance to do so.

Townsmen tended on the whole to be more affected by the Revolution than countrymen, even if well-off. Those who had held office under the old monarchy did not necessarily suffer: revolution and war created new posts to meet new needs and old *parlementaires* found they were needed to run the new judicial system. Contractors and financiers found new opportunities in a world of Revolutionary and wartime demand. In France as elsewhere, a last golden age was beginning for those who could make money while governments had still no effective means of taxing income. Poorer townsmen, though, may well have found that conscription for military service bore more heavily on them than on country-dwellers—partly because it was harder to enforce it in the countryside, where policing was hard and flight from conscription easier, and partly because probably the Directory and certainly the Napoleonic regime were willing to soft-pedal rather than provoke disaffection and possible resistance among those who produced the townsmen's food. In the towns—especially Paris —there was always a pool of impoverished and unemployed to be tapped fairly easily. Although we do not know the exact figures, it seems reasonable to assume that a townsman was more likely to be killed on military service as a result of the Revolution than was a countryman, unless the latter lived in a district where civil war had been a reality in 1793.

The towns are different in another way: it is there that the impact of the Revolution on women is easiest to observe. From the first year of the Revolution, women were in the forefront of bread riots, attacks on bakers' shops, *taxation populaire*, and so on. Townswomen were less likely to be wage-earners if they were married and had families than if they were spinsters (a huge population of servant-girls was the largest component among female wage-earners in Paris) but wives identified the Revolution with the promotion of the interests of the wage-earners to whom they were married—they were fairly consistently on the consumer side. Peasant women are both harder to discern in the records of the Revolution and less easy to relate categorically to the economy; they were often producers as well as consumers (to maintain that division, crude as it is), but their individual circumstances varied as much as those of their husbands; they might be so placed as hardly to need access to a market or they might be dependent upon the money they could earn as servants, labourers in the field, or as knitters or weavers in their own home, while their husbands worked their own (or someone else's) land. It seems a reasonable guess, though, that wherever the economic shoe pinched, women, in town and country alike, were likely to feel it more acutely and earlier than their menfolk.

Beyond this, the difference made by the Revolution to women is very hard to discern. In many ways the law's changes affected them more in principle than they did men. But such specific political and legal claims as were made on women's behalf had little success; the revolutionaries did not envisage female liberation. Nor, probably, did the over-whelming majority of women. In the deepest sense of striving to maintain the order they knew, albeit relieved of some of its disadvantages, women showed themselves time and again to be as conservative as their menfolk. In the narrowest and most political sense of the word, many of them went further; whatever the reason, the women of the villages and small towns of France emerged from the Revolution as church-goers, the supporters of the clergy, filling the parish church at mass while their menfolk drank at the *café* (the nineteenth-century descendent of the *cabarets* or dram-shops so often condemned in the parish *cahiers* of 1789, no doubt because the *curé* was there to help in the drafting). Perhaps this was because the Revolution often came to a community as an intrusion from the outside. Women rallied to its old centre, the church, voting with their knees at the altar-rail and confessional. The formal suffrage was denied to them—and to their successors until 1946—for the Revolution was very much a man's affair. Paradoxically, women may even have lost legal ground in it; there is evidence that some women took part in the assemblies which elected electors and drew up *cahiers* in 1789, acting in their right as property-owners.

The poorest women suffered most, both because they were

women, and therefore likely to be abandoned with their
children by their menfolk, and because they were poor. Those
—and there were many, perhaps a tenth of the population—
who always lived at the edge of destitution and starvation
under the old order experienced a change for the worse, hard
to conceive though that may be. The agencies for their relief
which existed before 1789 were suddenly swept away by the
ecclesiastical legislation of the Constituent Assembly. The
revolutionary assemblies then initiated work on new ways of
providing for the poor (as contemporary Englishmen were
doing) but little came of this. Meanwhile, every deterioration
in economic conditions hit the poorest harder than anyone
else. Destitute and unemployed men, if not physically in-
capacitated, might join the army or obtain employment
during spells of economic improvement; the old, the infirm,
the sick, the very young could not do this. Even among the
poorest, then, there are distinctions to be made.

Those who had bought land were probably net gainers
from the Revolution; they certainly were if they paid for it
in depreciated *assignats* after judicious currency speculation.
But the amount of property still held in tiny holdings, and
the extent to which the country-dweller had still to supplement
his earnings by casual labour and cottage industry suggest
that for many Frenchmen and Frenchwomen, life was not
much changed by the Revolution in the short run—and it
is the short run, of course, which matters to people, as opposed
to demographic statistics, for they are not there to witness
the improvements (or deteriorations) of the *longue durée*. The
majority of peasants lived in 1799 much as ten years earlier,
so far as their daily round went. Whether independent
exploiters, leasehold tenants, or share-croppers, they were
likely to be undercapitalized, working hard to achieve low
levels of production with outdated methods. Apart from the
disappearance of the ecclesiastical landlord, the rural order
often cannot have looked very different to them after ten years
so far as property-holding went; what was different were the
forms and legal institutions—there was no tithe, none of the
felt injustice of extra payments and fees of the seigneurial
system, no obligations in the manorial court. But the big house

had in most places the same family living in it as ten years earlier even if they did not use their old titles (that would come back a few years later). Nor, for all the important legal changes of the Constituent, did men's minds always keep up with them; the language of feudal relationships could still be found in use in parts of France in the twentieth century and local pressures still sometimes enforced collective usages long after their legal underpinning had been taken away.

The conservatism of so much local life appears, too, in the stability of the local élites who provided for so long the political fibre of France, the actual wielders of power with whom *représentants en mission*, Napoleonic prefects, and nine-teenth-century Ministers of the Interior of different political stamps had to grapple. These were the real directors of French life, their power sometimes shaken and in abeyance during the crisis of the Terror, but in many respects recovered and even strengthened in the long run, as they found themselves in a world where the defensive collectivity of the old rural community had been fractured and where their freedom to exploit their wealth was much greater. Here if anywhere, was the 'ruling class' of France.

It had long been a more complicated entity than could be adequately represented by the noble landowners who were its core. It is not easy to find clear categories to define it, whether those of legal status under the old order or of a particular relationship to the productive process under the new. The nobility itself, central to this nebulous group, was itself a complex entity; before 1789 the fact of legally noble status masked great varieties of privilege, wealth, economic function, and social power. This is one reason why it is hard to say anything very helpful about what happened to the 'nobility' during the Revolution. Another is the variety of different circumstances through which the Revolution was mediated. Tearing down coats-of-arms and breaking up family pews in parish churches might cause a stir, but even when this happened, many noble families did not suffer much. Revolutionary huffing and puffing is a poor guide, too: for all the Parisian rhetoric about 'aristocrats', it was not a word used only of the nobly-born. Yet the legal status of nobility and the privileges specifically associated with it do provide one safe generalization; these were abolished in the Revolution and this was an important landmark in the passage from one society to another, which some nobles felt deeply. The life-style of old France could not be revived once it had gone; a nobleman could not simply resume his traditional place in the society of his locality in 1815, even if his wealth remained intact and his property unmolested.

Not only is it hard to generalize, it is not easy to say much that is precise or personal about the fate suffered by the old rulers of France after 1789 unless they were individually damaged through confiscation, assault on their persons or property, imprisonment, emigration or—in the outstanding examples—by murder or execution. Even emigrants often maintained the family properties they should have lost by means of fictional or real transfers of ownership. For the most part, noble families sat it out, emerging at the end without old and sometimes valuable privileges, perhaps a little more self-consciously consolidated and aware of the fragility of social order and the need to defend religion and property. The removal of the formal distinction of nobility nonetheless left it easier for them to recognize themselves as belonging to the same camp as the legally non-noble who had shared through office and property in the possession of a directing role in local society even before 1789 and were, with them, the rulers of post-Revolutionary France. This amalgam may best be designated (in an eighteenth-century phrase which was to have its full exploitation by historians of nineteenth-century France) as the 'notables'. This word also provides a better thread than 'nobility' through the labyrinthine complications of the rich and varied world of social and legal power under the old monarchy. Formal nobility loomed very large in the eyes of contemporaries, of course, but actually denoted only a little of what was at stake in 1789. Noblemen might dominate the great councils and offices of State and fill the dioceses and great abbeys, but those who enjoyed these rewards were themselves drawn from only a tiny section of their order and the government of France required the acquiscence and participation of many non-nobles, as well.

As for economic domination, even before 1789 the majority of landowners were not noblemen, nor were all those who held seigneuries.

'Notables' seems a more helpful term than the seductive and much-used '*bourgeoisie*'. The office-holders and lawyers who made up so much of the dominant class before 1789 were not bourgeois in the classical Marxist sense of being owners of industrial or commercial capital. Indeed, very few Frenchmen were in that position. On the other hand, many owned land or property and in this sense they were capitalists, deeply interested in the maintenance of much of the existing order because of their stake in it, and aspiring to the rewards it offered. Great financiers and merchants sought titles; at the bottom end of the 'capitalist' class to which they belonged we must place the shopkeepers and master-craftsmen who were the backbone of the *sansculotte* movement. There were very few industrialists who looked consciously to a new order. These qualifications held for the revolutionary assemblies themselves. The men of the Constituent, Legislative, and Convention, were one after the other increasingly representative of the non-noble but property-owning, professional groups which were to rule France for the next century and were rarely great industrialists or financiers.

Mentality

Men's minds do not change overnight. In one part of the West in 1796 people saw an angel with tricolour wings: it is just as significant that the wings were those of an angel as that they bore the national colours of the new France. The angel was identified as a country girl of pro-revolutionary family murdered by royalists; soon there were miracles at the site of what was seen as her martyrdom. Republican ideology did not deny her the signs of sanctity traditionally associated with Christian martyrdom. The foundations of mentality rest in images, concepts, and language in which startling innovations stand out with much more obviousness than the tough, persisting old determinants of the way men and women look at the world. The violence of some extremists over symbols—

battlements, hatchments, weather-cocks, castellation, the *tutoyer*, the Phrygian caps of liberty—is only comprehensible if we grasp just how strong the obstacle to change presented by the inertia of ideas and symbols could be.

This was all the more true and important because most people could not read or write. As the growing flood of books and pamphlets before 1789 testifies, France probably contained more people able to read than any other European country. Yet about two-thirds of those who married did not sign their names in the register. The proportion was higher in the South than the North, a fact which should remind us also of the lack of homogeneity in French life before 1789. Its variety was sometimes expressed in spoken language, too. The Committee of Public Safety had to consider how to impose the use of French in some departments. French was the language of the printed culture on which the circulation of regulations and propaganda rested, as well as an ideological affirmation of national unity. Because of this, it is easy to overlook the persistence of local dialect and usage which was ignored by the official mythology but hardly disturbed by the educational innovations of the Revolution. In the 1860s there were still eighteen Departments in which almost all the communes were not French-speaking. The written language, of course, also exemplifies the weight of the past. The 1789 dictionary of the Academy bore few marks of revolutionary innovation—and this is not surprising, for it was the work of the *philosophe* academicians who had dominated that institution since the 1760s.

One of the major bodies of documentation for the understanding of the Revolution, the *cahiers de doléances*, shows this conservatism very deeply. To understand it, some attention has to be given to the way they were drawn up, for though they are written documents, their written form emerges from the depths of the spoken culture, as the earthiness of some of the language used in them well illustrates.

Each group of deputies to the Estates-General came with its own *cahier*, given to it by its electors. These were the documents sometimes called 'the general *cahiers*' but in the case of the Third Estate they had been drawn up only at the last stage of distillation which had begun at the level of individual parish, trade corporation, or town council. The clergy and nobility were relatively small bodies who could assemble as a whole in the town which was the centre of the electoral district, but there were too many *roturiers* for this. So they met in their parish churches to choose delegates and draw up their own 'preliminary' *cahiers*. These documents were then taken to the electoral assembly and in a measure— but only in a measure—were in due course absorbed into the general *cahiers*. The people who were handling them at that stage were far less representative of the mass of Frenchmen than those who had drawn them up. Consequently, the general *cahiers* tended to express more of what was wanted and feared by the educated, the literate, the better-off. Even the preliminary *cahiers*, too, do not always transmit the pure voice of the people (if such a thing were possible) because they had to be written down: the influence of the writer— priest, notary, schoolmaster—or of local bigwigs (*coqs du village*), or of 'model' *cahiers* circulating in the early months of 1789, all shaped their structure, themes, and language. Nevertheless, these facts are merely indications that we should be cautious, they need not obscure the fact that the *cahiers* of 1789, general and particular alike, provide a unique and matchless body of sources for the study of a national psychology at a crucial moment.

This said, what do they tell us? The most obvious facts which at once emerge from them are negative; the over-whelming majority of Frenchmen neither wanted nor expected revolutionary change in the foundations of social life. What they sought was correction, amelioration, reform, restoration. The predominant tone of the *cahiers* is conservative. Yet, paradoxically, they are packed with demands for innovations, though these are often couched in conservative terms. The demand for a constitution, for example, is frequent in the general *cahiers* of the Third Estate. Yet it is often coupled with the assertion, expressed or implied, that a constitution which once worked well has somehow been perverted or neglected. To use an English analogy, the constitutional aspirations of France in 1789 are much more reminiscent of

1640 than of 1832. There is a willingness to accept change, but rather for the upholding of old values and revitalizing of old institutions than for the assertion of new. The ideals of the Enlightenment find expression occasionally in a town where the local notables have had their say, but not in the rural documents which are the bulk of the *cahiers*.

At a more specific level, too, the ties with the past and with tradition are frequently apparent. Many of the clergy, for example, were willing to give up the curious system known as the 'free gift' (*don gratuit*) under which they had voted their own taxes, but wanted the *quid pro quo* that the Crown should take over the corporate debts of the Church. Their *cahiers*, too, were more emphatically conservative on the question of toleration and censorship of the press than any others, but they were at least well supported by the Third Estate; many of the laity made the point that though the privileges given to Protestants in 1787 might stand, the public manifestations of religion should be permitted only to the Roman Catholic faith.

The most striking and sweeping demands for change in the *cahiers* came in relation to taxes and the seigneurial order. But these were both areas in which the abuses of incoherences, irrationality, and privilege had been long and widely recognized. There was very little disagreement that something was very gravely wrong in both areas; all that was in question was the precise nature of what should be put in its place and what was said about this tended, like much else in the *cahiers*, to reflect the very specific and down-to-earth concerns of each community.

In the end, the Constituent Assembly went well beyond what the *cahiers* had asked for in most matters capable of generalized treatment. This is easy to understand; the Constituent was filled with men who not only represented entrenched privilege but who were drawn from circles favouring the most advanced views. Those from the Third Estate especially, were likely, by the mere fact of being chosen, to be exceptional men. On the whole, they were much more ready for changes than their constituents—and this held for many of the deputies of the privileged orders, too.

Popular behaviour in the Revolution bears this out. Once the great upheaval of 1789 was past and the structure which had maintained the power of the *seigneur* was overthrown, many communities proved very conservative, easily and quickly provoked to violence against the onset of further individualism. In particular, they soon began to interfere with the free circulation of grain and its unhindered distribution through the market. The *sansculottes*, too, might talk of dragging down the mighty from their seats and exalting the humble and meek, but they were indisposed to press further towards more fundamental change than might be possible within the framework of a democracy of small shopkeepers. (That in itself was, of course, a very radical aspiration indeed in the 1790s.) There were other such popular groups which showed their conservatism as the Revolution went on. The master-workers of the Lyons silk industry were artisans who sought to conserve their old restrictive organization of pre-Revolutionary days in spite of the Constituents' legislation. Their aim was to ensure the continuance of the minimum prices they had enjoyed, not the unchecked operation of *laissez-faire*. Such men were certainly revolutionaries, in the sense that their action had made the overthrow of the old order possible (indeed, they had been vital), but they were also true conservatives, men of the old order—and hardly surprisingly so, since they were born and brought up under it.

In their respect for the sanctity of property the *sansculottes* were at one with the members of the successive National Assemblies. The Constituent had in 1789 declared property to be a natural and imprescriptible right to be interfered with only in times of emergency and with due compensation. The aborted Constitution of 1793 maintained this and thus registered the Convention's adoption of the same views. This commitment to property illuminates the meaning attached by the new rulers of France to 'equality' (which was not declared an imprescriptible right in 1789 when all citizens were declared equal in law, but only achieved this status in 1793). The results of this respect for property were very important. When, finally, the Convention went so far as to declare that the lands of emigrants and suspects might be seized, it was only as punishment; they were guilty of an offence which merited sequestration without compensation. Yet the lands thus acquired were not to remain in the hands of the State and thus to be socialized, but were to be transferred to smallholders, so broadening and reinforcing the property-owning interest. If the three revolutionary assemblies were consistent about anything, it was that restraints on the enjoyment and exploitation of property should be removed. This was what the final abolition of 'feudal' forms in 1793 offered. Even under the Convention, when the *levée en masse* in principle placed property at the service of the State and transport and food-supplies were requisitioned, the justification was an emergency (it requisitioned the person of the citizen, too, if need be, and the greater interference included the lesser). This measure marks the high tide of the success of those Parisian leaders who were most egalitarian (as did the *Maximum*) but even with support for their aims on the Committee of Public Safety itself they could not obtain more than a temporary interference with the rights of property to meet a crisis.

Continuity of religion

The importance of mental continuities may be clearest in the sphere of religion. At the institutional and legal level—even at the economic—very grave ruptures in the religious history of France are obvious during the 1790s. The Church blessed with *Te Deums* the first acts of the Constituent, yet under the Directory, France had neither an established Church nor public financial support for any sect. The Roman Catholic monopoly, infringed even under the old order, had ceased. The Revolution had brought a startlingly complete toleration in principle—'no one', said the Declaration of the Rights of Man and the Citizen in a revealing phrase, 'should be molested for his opinions, *even* his religious ones' (*même religieuses*) provided that public order was not endangered. An end had come, too, to the practical interlacing of religious and secular institutions and life at all levels, from marriage to litigation over wills. Perhaps this was to most

Frenchmen one of the most obvious changes of the whole Revolution. Finally, there had been a great disendowment.

This was an institutional earthquake. Cumulatively, such changes shattered an age-old framework. Contemporaries did not underrate their importance. It is worth remarking, though, that not all the detailed and specific manifestations of this upheaval were unprecedented or undesired. Some— even if only a few and even if only early in the Revolution —were not necessarily repugnant even to very traditionally-minded clergy. The seizure of Church property did not irritate all Catholics; there was an old and respectable view that the Church should enjoy the usufruct of its wealth but that endowment was not essential to it. Ecclesiastical administration was not thought by all clergymen to be in principle beyond the proper scope of secular authority; since Carolingian times, the kings of France had regulated benefices or the working of religious communities when they had thought it proper to do so. As for the deeper doctrinal issues raised by the need to redefine the relationship of Church and State, Jansenist clergy saw no difficulty in submission to the temporal authority in everything except the administration of the sacraments and the preaching of the Gospel, while Gallicans who could not go so far as this could still hope to accommodate their old traditions within the new forms provided by the national State; in 1790 many of them hoped that the Pope would sanction the Civil Constitution of the Clergy and resented the dilemma in which he had placed them by refusing to do so. Finally, even among the French episcopate, aristocratic and privileged as it was, there was support for ecclesiastical reform. Few regretted the abolition of useless benefices, the levelling and rationalization of stipends, a guarantee of a decent income for the parish priest, the redefinition of diocesan boundaries. It is not too much to say that there was visible in virtually the whole Clerical Order at Versailles in 1789 some willingness to welcome a reorientation of the Church back towards the ideals of apostolic simplicity.

Much of this touches on questions of mentality, in the first place, among the clergy. The professional religious are by trade a vocal and often eloquent tribe and we have easier access to their minds than to those of their flock. About the laity, it is harder to speak with confidence. It seems certain, nevertheless, that the picture once held of a France suddenly and perhaps mortally wounded in its faith by the Revolution is over-simple. This view has been summed up in the word 'de-Christianized', an expression which was created by a nineteenth-century bishop to characterize the growing secularization he saw about him and feared, but has been applied in a different sense to the Revolution by some historians. They take it to indicate the acts of those extreme revolutionaries who wrecked churches, desecrated sacred symbols, and outraged priests, doing all this consciously as an anti-religious act. Neither in the sense that they predominated in the Revolutionary years, for they were always a minority, nor in the sense that France was paganized as a result can she be said to have been 'de-Christianized' by the work of these men.

Such evidence as we have of decline in religious practice points to a decisive point having been reached perhaps a half-century or so before the Revolution. Somewhere in the middle decades of the eighteenth century there begins to appear a decline in attendance at mass, in presentations for confirmation and even in monastic vocations which is the evidence of a deep change in religious outlook. Institutions of laymen which were explicitly religious in purpose and origin—the pious and charitable fraternities of the South, for example, which more and more grew to resemble secular bodies like masonic lodges or cultural societies—show a creeping secularization in the second half of the century. It is a complex change, more noticeable among men than women and in some dioceses rather than others, more easily tested in some ways than others, but one whose importance it is hard to gainsay. As for the centre of intellectual life, the phenomenon of the worldly clergy of fashionable Paris and the scepticism of its *salons* has never been under-emphasized. Against this background, it is reasonable to suggest that changes in religious practice which came after 1789 either intensified established trends or can be accounted for by the simple facts of disruption and upheaval which left so many churches deserted in the middle of the 1790s.

It is worth bearing in mind, too, that even some of the religious innovations of the Revolution, superficially startling as they are, are evidence of persistent and felt religious needs. The angel with tricolour wings appeared because angels were *known* by many Frenchmen to appear at important crises; miracles occurred at sites hallowed by the martyrdom of revolutionaries as they had occurred for centuries at the sites of Christian martyrdoms or the pagan shrines which antedated them. The language of 'fraternity', so much abused by revolutionary orators, was not strange to those who had grown used to the word in a Christian context by preachers; even the 'Supreme Being' which was the object of the official cult launched by Robespierre a few weeks before his downfall testified to the need for a religious focus for emotion and zeal, and was expressed in language and symbols rich with associations likely to appeal to the Catholic mind.

The Continuity of the Counter-Revolution

Religious continuity in the Revolution is not always so discreetly masked as in such manifestations as these. It is revealed also by the bloody acts which men were willing to embark upon in the name of religion (though it must sometimes only have salved their consciences over their less admissible motives). They ran from the violent outbreaks of Protestant–Catholic hatred which began early in the Revolution, to the fighting of the civil war, the *Vendée*, the *Chouannerie*, and the long-rumbling ulcer of royalism in the West. This bloodshed nourished the roots of the Counter-Revolution.

There is something misleading though, about that name, for it suggests response—a reply to the Revolution—rather than autonomous existence. In fact, the Counter-Revolution anticipated the Revolution. The paradox at the Revolution's birth is that it erupted because of resistance to innovation by the ministers of the old monarchy—'the noble revolt', the 'aristocratic resurgence', and many other names have been given to what happened. Such labels take us only a little way towards understanding what they summarize; they focus too narrowly upon the defence of privilege by a particular social group. It is perfectly permissible to use such labels for different aspects of events well before 1789. What happened that year, though, was really the defeat of a counter-revolutionary offensive begun in 1788.

Opposition to reform went back to the 1770s, when the Chancellor Maupeou gave a terrible shock to the *Parlements* by dispensing with them. In the end, nonetheless, he failed; next came Turgot's unsuccessful reforms. Calonne's 'new deal' of 1787 was from one point of view only the latest in a long series of such attempts. Practically speaking, those who opposed such changes advocated the maintenance of a restricted monarchy (some partisans of privilege in 1789 wished that *de facto* limitations which the monarchy had accepted because of its entanglement with the social order be formulated *de jure*) and the maintenance of particularism, corporatism, and localism. The Counter-Revolution was therefore anti-absolutist and anti-centralist. Parallel to this current flowed another, restricted more narrowly to a section of the clergy (among whom it gained ground especially after the edict of toleration of 1787) and a few devout laymen. These people saw the reforming tendencies of the monarchy not merely as inimical to the institutional independence of the Church, but as the expression of the secularizing and sceptical trend of the era which was also expressed in such steps as the ministerial relaxation of censorship. From thinking of this sort was ultimately to grow a justification of counter-revolution as one pole of the eternal antagonism between religion and paganism, spiritual and secular, established truth and subversive error. Before 1789, though, this idea was not much taken up by men of affairs, but was reserved to clergymen and cranks.

The crystallization of such attitudes into a cause was achieved in 1788 and 1789. The first marker is the decision to give to the Third Estate a representation in the Estates-General equal to the other two orders combined. This produced a notable, published protest to the King signed by almost all the princes of the Blood. It set out explicitly and with some perceptiveness the general issues and dangers for the privileged which lay behind the decision. It also hinted, not very subtly or discreetly, at the possibility of a new divergence between the interests of the Crown and those of the nobility; this was to become a reality a couple of years later, when the leaders of the emigration (among them the King's brothers) never hesitated to endanger or embarrass the royal family in pursuit of their own objectives. For some of the counter-revolutionaries at least, Louis XVI had become by 1791 at best a helpless king in toils, at worst a renegade.

The turning-point for the Counter-Revolution, after which it had either to accept the Revolution or be prepared to turn to armed opposition, was the session of 23 June 1789. To a remarkable degree, the programme of reforms then announced remained the charter of the Counter-Revolution. When the fall of the Bastille followed, the first emigrants left. Among them was Artois, the King's brother, and those who joined him were the first open counter-revolutionaries. Conservatives who remained in the Constituent resisted major innovations, but showed some skill in not entangling themselves with rearguard actions on behalf of discredited causes; the *parlements* disappeared almost undefended. The practical decentralization and disintegration of government and the collapse of the royal administrative system in 1789 and 1790 in fact suited many conservatives. Such resistance as had been shown, for example in Brittany, to centralization schemes under the old order died down somewhat in spite of the legislation of the Constituent because the practical impact of the new governmental structures was for a long time so slight; meanwhile, the new administrators of local government elected by the local notables enjoyed remarkable autonomy.

An indication that trouble might lie ahead, though, was already available in the anti-Protestant movements of the countryside in some parts of the South in 1790: these occurred even before the upheaval brought to almost every rural parish by the clerical oaths. That upheaval implied that, as the restraints on armed resistance crumbled, the temptation to turn to it would become irresistible because of the possibilities of widespread popular support. Soon—the war, once more, was the cause—foreign support became available (though not, it must be said, always on terms which suited the leaders of the emigration who were the custodians of the monarchic cause after the deposition of Louis XVI). Gradually, the crusading Counter-Revolution brought about a transformation in the mentality of the intransigent emigrant nobility; the tone of French aristocratic life after the Restoration of 1815 was to be quite different from that of the frivolous courtiers of Marie Antoinette's circle. (For that matter, it was to be quite different from that of her personal enemies; her husband's brother Artois, left the country notorious for his vice and scepticism, to return a quarter of a century later a religious bigot.)

Yet once the crisis of 1793 was passed, the Counter-Revolution turned out to be in every immediate and practical sense a failure except in so far as it forced the governments of the Directory and Napoleon to tacit recognition that parts of France were not governable against their will. The first Consul was clear-sighted about this, as the Concordat of 1801 shows. This restored France to the Roman fold, albeit at the sacrifice neither of the Revolutionary land settlement nor of the principle of toleration. The acceptability of this solution and the new strength soon shown by the French Church are the best testimony to the enduring power of Catholic sentiment in France; it had, moreover, been strengthened in some classes and communities by the symbolic value which came to be attached to renewed Christian religious activity as the sign that a period of uncertainty was over. But the Concordat was not the triumph of the Counter-Revolution, as the fate of what was called 'the little church' (*la petite église*), the following of those non-juring bishops who refused to accept it, showed.

Nor did the Counter-Revolution triumph in 1815. The Bourbon line came back then, but on terms, to a constitutional monarchy, with the essential rights of 1789 guaranteed, the revolutionary establishment undisturbed except for a few hard-core regicides, the land settlement untouched, and no return to the old localism and corporatism. Though a more blatantly reactionary programme still seemed feasible to some and lingered as a serious possibility as late as the 1870s (thereafter it was merely intellectual indulgence), the Counter-Revolution's practical effect in French history was as negligible as its mythological and intellectual importance was great. Practical conservatism after 1815 increasingly flowed away from it and into the channels favoured by the notables who emerged triumphant from the Revolution.

Continuity and discontinuity

So much evidence exists of the essential continuity of the processes of the 1790s with the French past that it is necessary from time to time to make conscious adjustments in our usual way of looking at the Revolution. Instead of seeing it only as a great innovating agent (which it was), whose significance lies in the wholly new forces it brought into French and world history (as it does for the most part) we ought to recall its more indirect influence. It is also made easier the course of in-novations already under way. Its essential nature explains this: it was a great release, a taking-off of a lid, an explosive liber-ation of the pressure of forces generated deep within French society. The effect of this sudden, disorganizing outburst was, for the most part, to make easier changes which pointed the way towards a new sort of society, some of them positively accelerating advance in that direction. But many of the hitherto-suppressed forces seem, on closer inspection, to have much more of the old about them than of the new. Even the conscious substantive changes of Revolutionary law-making had precedents; the men who abolished guilds, reformed weights and measures, formulated new judicial and penal codes, were those who had for years worked away at plans for such changes within the bureaucracy of the old monarchy. They were men of the old order, like most of the legislators they worked for. The impact of the Great Revolution here, as elsewhere, took time to mature; a new generation had to grow up under its institutions before we can detect substantial changes in mentality and behaviour.

5

The Revolution at large

In one important sense the Revolution is now more alive than ever, for in the last fifty years or so the ideals of nationalism and liberation, the inspiring themes of 1789, have had greater success than ever before. They won great victories in Europe and the Americas between 1815 and 1919, and have since rolled outwards. Nation-making is still going on in Africa and Asia, and new aims have been found for liberation in western countries. Speeches about the emancipation of women in the United Nations General Assembly may remain only lip-service but their hypocrisy shows the need even in traditional societies to pay tribute to that cause. Meanwhile, in the European world an increasing search for new frontiers of liberation goes on; the drop-out has become a familiar sight, schoolchildren are encouraged to assert their rights against parents and society alike, and the seeding of new anti-industrial communes is so normal as to be unremarkable. Even the dreary strains of 'We shall overcome' mysteriously show the indisputable and intoxicating power of the dream of liberation. The men of '89 and '94 would no more recognize all of their modern ideological descendants than would the latter readily acknowledge them among spiritual ancestors they revere. Yet even the most bizarre gestures of modern liberation fall out from the revolutionary tradition which made abstract human liberty an unquestionable value, and it is still widely believed that nationhood provides the only political door through which liberty may be approached.

For decades, the ideas of 1789 wore better than any of their rivals. Though the way they developed could not have been anticipated either in its details or its forms by the Revolutionary generation, that these ideas were quickly sensed to transcend their own time is clear. The armies of France marched about Europe until 1814 with the comforting thought that however much pillage, torture, rape, and murder might accompany their progress, so did the cause of humanity itself. Mirabeau had told his fellow-legislators at the outset that they could give laws to the whole universe if they wished. In 1791 a foreign observer and sympathizer, Tom Paine, linked the Revolution to its American predecessor as the embodiment of 'a system of principles as universal as it is true'. Goethe's observation at the battle of Valmy, the turning-point of the first Prussian invasion of France, that on that day began a new era in the history of the world, is perhaps no longer familiar enough to schoolboys for yet another recollection of it not to be justified. In his last speech in the Convention, Robespierre affirmed his conviction that it was the glory of the Revolution that it was the first ever to be founded on the theory of the rights of humanity, and that without the love of humanity to inspire it, all that had happened would have been just another of history's crimes. Many more such witnesses could be cited. Perhaps it is enough to recall that those who feared revolutionary France, too, sensed that what faced them was more than just a powerful and predatory State; they recognized in their opponent the embodiment of universally subversive principle.

Such views were to contribute to a rich and long-growing mythology of the Revolution. They were one expression of the way in which very quickly, the revolutionary influence was felt everywhere. Yet this was not just because of the inherent charm or power of revolutionary ideas. It was also likely from the outset that any large upheaval in France would have an effect beyond her borders, whatever its nature. The question of 'why' what happened in France had effects abroad cannot be easily separated from 'how', but it makes things easier if we start with the predisposing facts which were bound to make revolution in France a potent international influence.

Why a French revolution mattered abroad

In the simplest sense, what happened in France mattered because France was a great power. She had few equals anywhere, and in the Atlantic world, none. China, a greater State than any European, was almost inconceivably remote from day-to-day diplomatic calculations; she could be ignored. Russia, though incontestably a giant, was still in 1789 an eastern European giant; her power was feared, but its limits and range were still uncertain (though Russian soldiers had marched into Berlin in 1760 and a Russian fleet had made its appearance in the Mediterranean for the first time ten years later). France was indisputably the greatest State in the world formed from western Christendom.

Her power rested on her large population, on a century-old tradition of military and diplomatic expertise, and on the geography which committed her to Atlantic, Mediterranean, and continental roles. French economic resources were great, even if it was not easy to mobilize them; by eighteenth-century standards she was a rich country. In particular, she was the predominant land power in western Europe. Since the stabilization of her main land frontiers early in the century, the settlement of old disputes in Italy, and the acquisition of Lorraine and Corsica, France enjoyed something of a political hegemony there.

For a century or more, the power generated by such facts as these made French policy of especial interest to every other European State. Among them, the Habsburg monarchy stood out, the inheritor of a long tradition of rivalry with the kings of France, though since the middle of the century, hostility between the two monarchies was in abeyance. By 1789, one old area of Austro-French conflict, Italy, had been neutralized for forty years. A Franco-Austrian alliance existed and an Austrian queen sat on the throne of France. The change this implied in Germany and central Europe should have released French diplomatic and military energies for deployment elsewhere, yet the alliance came to be unpopular, for it appeared to cost France more than she gained. Another major power with whom France's relations were bound to be important was the United Kingdom. Since the days of Louis XIV a nearly worldwide competition between the French and British for colonies and trading advantages had gone on until, seemingly, settled by British victory in 1763. Yet though humiliated by the loss of Canada and forced into second place in India, the French monarchy seized the chance of a tit-for-tat in 1778 and joined the rebellious American colonists against its old rival. Great Britain soon seemed reduced indeed. With virtually all west and north Europe in arms against her, she extracted herself from danger at the cost of acknowledging the independence of the new United States of America. Peace restored Anglo-French relations to a formally friendly footing —there was a commercial treaty to prove it—but they were again threatened in 1789 by a European irritant. The internal troubles of the Dutch republic had tempted French dabbling there and an Anglo-Prussian alliance ostentatiously provided a shield for the republic against intervention by any other power.

The effect of this was to link issues in western and eastern Europe. For nearly half-a-century Prussia and Austria had been rivals in Germany. They had once settled their differences by despoiling Poland, in collaboration with the Russians. French policy in the Netherlands, involving as it did the Habsburg monarchy both as an ally and as the possessor of what is now Belgium, was to have repercussions and implications as far away as the Vistula, therefore. Elsewhere, two other States which had an especial interest in French policy round off the picture. One was Spain, the other considerable monarchy ruled by a Bourbon (other branches of the family were installed at Naples and Parma), and an ally of France in colonial conflict with England. France and Spain were linked formally by the 'Family Compact', a treaty last renewed in 1761 which proclaimed in grandiose language that the enemy of one branch of the House of Bourbon was the enemy of both and that France and Spain would act as a single power. The Ottoman empire was the other State with which France was particularly connected, both by a tradition of maintaining Turkish power in eastern Europe to offset that of the Habsburgs (a tradition whose weakening after the

Austrian alliance was much regretted by some French diplomats) and through the development of the Levant trade from which Marseilles had so prospered in the eighteenth century.

In short, the French monarchy was directly and closely involved with worldwide issues and many other powers; any change in its government could therefore have far-reaching implications.

Yet there was still more than this to French influence abroad. It can be summed up in the title of a book published by an Italian in 1772: *l'Europe Française*. Both the title and choice of language express concisely another fact of great importance, France's cultural preponderance. Its greatest years were passing by 1789, yet it was even then immense and practically very important. It had begun with the assertion of the superiority of French civilization and style under Louis XIV. The prestige he cultivated was testified to by many imitations of Versailles in the next fifty years and by the enthronement of the French language as the first common language of educated men after Latin. French was also established as the language of diplomacy, and to this practical supremacy and the cultural magnificence to which it gave access was soon added the glamour and glitter of advanced ideas; France was for two-thirds of the eighteenth century the source—or at least the conduit—of most of what was new and significant in European thought. The generation of the Encyclopedia reaped the benefit of a linguistic hegemony. In an especially articulate era France became the supreme embodiment of the values and teaching of the Enlightenment, the barbarities of much of her government and social life notwithstanding. The growth of printing and publication which marked the century owed much to the prevalence of French as a literary medium (and reinforced it, too) and encouraged the persistence of this predominating cultural orientation among the élites of Europe. It was bound to make them especially attentive towards what was happening in France in 1789—especially when it became clear that much of what was going on could be understood and interpreted by the revolutionary generation in terms of the

Enlightenment values and goals which many of these élites shared.

Power, the ramifications of international interests, and the cultural leadership implied in the words *Europe française* may sufficiently explain the predisposition of the Revolution to make a big impact outside France. But it was soon asserted that another essential ingredient was the subversive potential of revolutionary ideas and institutions themselves. This was what Frenchmen themselves had in mind when they began in the later 1790s to speak of their country as *la grande nation*; they gloried in the innovation forced on others, just as the old order had gloried in the consciousness of diffusing French civilization through the prestige of the monarchy. It was true that they did not always understand what the ultimate effect of such innovation would be, but in almost every country in 1789 there existed conflicts or potential conflicts which made it easier for Frenchmen to believe that they had something relevant to offer. This was the first instance of the universalizing of a political ideology as a guide to diplomatic and military policy and it was soon to prove as productive of misunderstanding, disappointment, and frustration as the later export of European institutions and ideas to the non-European world in the last phase of overseas imperialism, or the imposition of communism in some countries after 1945. Yet there was a sort of plausibility about the revolutionaries' perspective upon other countries which can still be felt; even in recent years historians have tried to justify general interpretations of the politics of the later eighteenth century with such labels as 'the age of the democratic revolution'.

Such attempts usually fall into the same error as did some of the evangelists of exported revolution in the 1790s; they over-simplify the conflicts to which the revolutionaries looked so hopefully. These were of very different types and significance. Some—in parts of the Habsburg dominions, for example—had their roots in the policies of reforming monarchies which stirred up animosities among their subjects. Sometimes, they registered cultural changes such as, for example, were shown by a reassertion of religious and spiritual values in parts of Germany in the 1780s against those of the more utilitarian and mechanistic apostles of the Enlightenment. Sometimes such conflicts were only comprehensible within very specific historical traditions—the struggle of republicans and Orangists in Holland, for example, or the stirring of demands for the 'emancipation' of religious dissenters in the United Kingdom. Sometimes, too, there were signs of national resentments against alien rule (the implications of the American War of Independence had not gone unnoticed).

Whether or not they read the signs correctly, all this provided a potential the revolutionaries were almost bound to exploit, even if not very consciously at first. It helped enormously that the Revolution quickly threw up a framework of interpretation, a language, and an ideology into which most political facts could be fitted. Thus the impact of revolutionary ideas was to be not unlike that exercised by Marxism a century or so later; both provided toolkits of ideas and myths which made it possible to simplify issues and so to act effectively. Of course, this did not mean that the groups and interests which seemed *prima facie* likely to sympathize with France in fact always did so. All it meant was that in almost every country some people soon came to look to France with hope, some with fear and loathing, but that almost everyone also came to believe that French politics were for good or ill relevant to their own. The upshot was that the Revolution in the end became an issue in politics almost everywhere. This was not without its ironies and paradoxes. England was France's most enduring opponent for the whole revolutionary era, though in England men already enjoyed many of the liberties for which the revolutionaries claimed to be struggling.

Spreading the Revolution

Not since the era of the Spanish Reconquest or the Reformation had Europe seen so conscious a diffusion of ideas and institutions as the Revolution brought about. They were vigorously exported by journalism, diplomacy, and brute force. Most French politicians considered the ideological attitudes of other countries as of great importance and did not assess policy simply on diplomatic or military grounds, though at some moments the missionary impulse was more evident than at others. Some uttered warnings, too. Early in the Revolution Robespierre had told his countrymen not to misinterpret in terms of their own struggles events in Brabant, where a revolt by the Belgian subjects of the Austrian emperor was in full swing; later, in opposing the war, he gave them an even more prescient warning—unheeded— that armed missionaries were never likely to prove popular. In those early days, propaganda and sympathetic rhetoric were still more a matter of individual and private effort than of official policy, yet in the slow redirection of French foreign policy towards the positive promotion of the Revolution's interests which followed, there was nothing illogical; the cause of the Revolution quickly became inseparable from that of France and the national interest was redefined accordingly. One symbolic change in phraseology suggests the shifts of implication which took place almost unwilled; the King of France became 'King of the French' in the new Constitution and his office was declared to exist solely in virtue of laws made by the nation. Whatever this might mean in domestic politics it surely entailed an end to the old dynastic view of foreign policy.

That Revolution had special consequences for French foreign policy began to appear even under the Constituent. Three episodes, in particular, helped to reveal it. The first was one of the earliest demonstrations of what the reorganization of France around the principle of national sovereignty might imply to foreigners. The August decrees on the feudal regime clearly applied to French nationals; did it follow that they applied to those who had never been subjects of the King of France, yet who were seigneurial proprietors of lands within France? The issue arose over sovereign German territorial princes with fiefs on the left bank of the Rhine in Alsace. National sovereignty, it was resolved, overrode the traditional law (of which respect for the seigneurial principle was, of course, a part) of Europe as well as that of France in this matter. The second question was that of the papal

enclaves of which Avignon was the most important. Some
of the inhabitants, possibly a majority, clamoured for their
incorporation in France and the ending of the Pope's government. Blood was shed; the Parisian supporters of the would-be
French Avignonese urged their case. The affair dragged on,
complicated politically by the contemporaneous negotiation
with Rome over the Civil Constitution of the Clergy. In the
end, the outcome was again in favour of national sovereignty,
though this time asserted in a more blunt and alarming form,
that of self-determination; if subjects wished to transfer their
allegiance from their sovereign, it seemed, then the French
government was prepared to support their right to do so at
the cost of existing law, prescription, treaty, or any other
restraint. Of course, the issue was still not completely and
starkly faced; it was blurred in that the enclaves were deep
in French territory and the Pope (as later statesmen might
have put it) did not have many divisions. The monarchy,
too, had in the past sometimes shown itself willing to handle
relations with Rome pretty briskly when it felt like it. Still,
a new doctrine had made its appearance in European
diplomatic practice.

The third important episode in the evolving relations of
France with other countries which helped to crystallize a
characteristically revolutionary stance in foreign policy
involved quite different considerations. In 1790, it looked as
if Great Britain and Spain might go to war over their con-
tending claim in Nootka Sound, far off in the remote North-
West of America. Given the Family Compact, was not France
bound to join in on the side of Spain? The outcome of the
squabble was peaceful, in that French diplomacy was brought
to bear so as to persuade the Spanish to give way, but the
material outcome was not all that mattered. The crisis forced
Frenchmen to consider what respect they owed to inherited
obligations from pre-Revolutionary days. It was especially
galling, of course, that the particular treaty in question was
by its name and nature so evocative of the diplomacy of
dynasties. The age of the diplomacy of peoples, some thought,
should now begin.

These three episodes all sharpened a growing feeling that

a revolutionary France needed a quite new kind of foreign policy, not merely to protect and uphold new interests created by the Revolution, but one which rested on theoretical and juridical foundations explicitly different from those of the old monarchy. This feeling, nurtured by some radical politicians in the Legislative Assembly, combined with domestic developments already indicated to lead to the French declaration of war on Austria in 1792.

So much later history was to flow from this act, which opened an era of change throughout Europe, that it is worthwhile to glance ahead for a moment. To take the long view, it was the beginning of twenty-two years during which France was almost continuously at war with at least one other European power and often with several. Of the most important, Russia, Austria, Prussia, and Spain all fought against her. Yet Spain and Prussia were at other times her allies and Russia and Austria co-operated with her for substantial periods. Great Britain alone remained an almost implacable enemy, making peace only once, and keeping up its guard when it did so. The vast involvement of the major powers was accompanied by the entanglement of many smaller countries and petty sovereigns in France's affairs. All the Italian and most German states (there were some hundreds of the latter in 1792) were eventually sucked into the diplomatic and military wake of the Revolution. All Italy and much of Germany was invaded by French armies and long occupied—some areas more than once. So were the Dutch Republic, Spain and Portugal. Other French armies penetrated deep into the Ottoman and Russian empires, at one time seizing Egypt, and at another occupying Moscow. Two popes were taken off to captivity by French soldiers and when this happened for the second time, the Temporal Power was abolished, the territories of the former Papal states becoming new departments of the new French Empire.

This directs our attention towards a second fact. Besides invasion, and material and human destruction on a huge scale, this era of turmoil was marked by great territorial and institutional changes. These did not always endure. Satellite States set up first as republics by the Directory and Consulate and then as monarchies under the French Empire tended sooner or later to collapse. The wraithlike Duchy of Warsaw disappeared like many other French creations in the peace settlements of 1815. There were some important restorations, then, too. But much was never revived. The old republics of Genoa and Venice did not come back (though the second briefly reappeared for the last time in 1848). The Papal enclaves disappeared for ever. The old Dutch Republic had gone, too, replaced by a new kingdom of the Netherlands incorporating it with the old Austrian provinces of Belgium. This was not to last for long but in the end two new constitutional monarchies were to be the result, not a revived United Provinces. Above all, although the Temporal Power of the Pope had been restored in 1815 and the Legations put back under his rule, the Holy Roman Empire had gone and with it much of the ancient German polity. In its stead was a new, simplified Germany, organized as a confederation and effectively dominated by Austria. These were the main territorial and diplomatic consequences of the Revolution in Europe. There were still more beyond the seas.

Rearrangements on this scale suggest the scope of the Revolution's impact well enough, but are still not the whole story. Revolutionary example, propaganda, and inspiration awoke responses among sympathizers in many countries; they were called 'Jacobins' in the 1790s by their governments, and if their countries were invaded, they (at least at the outset, though some of them learnt better) welcomed the French and provided them with collaborators and Quislings. Occupation sometimes turned them into opponents and resistance fighters; in this way they were supported by many of their countrymen who, whatever their ideological sympathies or lack of them, bore the immediate impact of French presence in the forms of rape, pillage, drumhead justice, impositions, conscription, and shortages. From the experience of French rule came the political education of two generations of Europeans.

The export of Revolution 1792–1814

French rule was not a constant. It changed frequently in its nature and aims in twenty-two years, often because of the twists and turns of international affairs. The French declaration of war against Austria was followed within a few months by a Prussian declaration of war on France. In February 1793, the French added to their enemies by declaring war on Great Britain and the Dutch Republic and a month later on Spain. A number of minor states (of which Sardinia and Naples were the most important) later completed the array of France's enemies which has traditionally been called the 'First Coalition'. Even before the end of 1792, the French had indicated that the development of a revolutionary foreign policy embracing much more than the simple cause of national security (which, it might be argued, was still the theoretical basis of the ultimatum to the Emperor early in 1792) was under way. They did this in decrees which offered the help of the Republic to any people striving to achieve freedom from their rulers and ordered French generals to proclaim the sovereignty of the people and abolish existing authorities in any territories they invaded. At the time, such policies could only realistically be applied to Belgium but they were ominous. The Republic's generals were also ordered to sequester the property of sovereigns and corporations in the territories they occupied; this announced another aspect of revolutionary policy which was to loom much larger in the future; victory was to be made to pay for itself in booty. The trial and execution of the King gave, as it were, an extra edge to these pronouncements. According to your point of view, there was now much to be hoped for or feared from France; relations with her would entail much more than the calculation of old-fashioned diplomatic advantage and interest.

Though there were bad moments, France survived the war of the First Coalition and made successful treaties of peace with all her enemies except Great Britain. In the war and these treaties, much of the story of the next twenty years was prefigured. Deliberately, the Republic employed subversion and propaganda. The arrival of French armies was followed by the proclamation of the Rights of Man and the formal abolition of feudalism—policies with widely differing impacts, of course, given the very different circumstances of different countries. Nevertheless, the broad effect was towards the diffusion of institutions on French lines and certainly towards the abolition of the past. In 1799, for example, when the Republic faced a new hostile coalition, the former Austrian Netherlands, Savoy, Nice, and Piedmont had all become French departments under the municipal law of France, their former rulers deposed (the king of Sardinia had retired to Sardinia, though the Emperor, of course, remained in Vienna). In addition, the Dutch Republic of the United Provinces had been replaced by a Batavian Republic, the Swiss cantons by a Helvetic Republic, while most of the rest of Italy was divided between a 'Cisalpine' Republic in the North, a 'Roman' in the centre, and a 'Parthenopean' in the South.

Other satellite republics had already come and gone and none of them was to endure, but the pattern of the deliberate imposition of French institutions either by absorption within the French state itself or through the creation of satellites with Frenchified constitutions went on under the Consulate and Empire, when they had the additional purpose of providing patronage for distribution to Bonaparte's family and lieutenants. The satellite states became monarchical; Madrid and Naples received French kings, while the Papal territories became imperial departments. In Germany, notable reallocations of territory took place in consequence of the distribution of former ecclesiastical lands, and a new kingdom of Westphalia made its appearance. The upshot overall was that millions of Europeans lived for periods of years at a time—and sometimes almost continually for nearly twenty years—under French laws and institutions, and officials either French or sympathetic to French methods. Thousands served in the French army or in the forces of satellite states armed, organized, and drilled on French lines. This amounted to a very great diffusion of French ideas, institutions, and methods.

It is impossible to generalize about the results because of differences in local circumstances and French policy; seigneurial dues, for example, were not as completely swept away by the Napoleonic years in Germany as they had been by the satellite republics of Italy. It is reasonable, nonetheless, to distinguish three responses which were almost universally observable. In the first place chronologically, there was often sympathy and admiration, and it was not always wholly sacrificed by the actual exploitation of their satellites in which the Directory and later the Empire indulged, and by the indiscipline of French commanders and their soldiers. Second, there was an equally widespread sentiment of repulsion and resistance, notable above all among the displaced possessing classes and—before the Concordat—among the clergy of satellites and occupied territories alike. The third widespread response was that of the rural population of almost every country; whatever the theoretical benefits they might derive from the implementation of French legislation, they nearly always turned at some point to open resistance, sporadic though it might be. Except in northern Germany, the peasantry were everywhere in Europe the most persistently alienated of the Revolution's potential supporters, whatever the benefits the new order might appear to bring them at first sight. The beginnings of a story of resistance are to be found in the *barbets* of the Piedmontese Alps in 1795; popular resistance flared up again in Lombardy in the following year, at the onset of the armies of the Second Coalition in northern and southern Italy in 1799, in the Abruzzi in 1806, in Spain two years later, in the Tyrol in 1809, and finally in Russia in 1812. It was among the better-off and the urbanized that the supporters of the French were to be found, not in the countryside which they formally liberated from 'feudalism'.

Of course, not all townsfolk found French hegemony acceptable. In particular, those areas whose commerce or industry were sacrificed to French designs were irritated. One of the most conservative aspects of French revolutionary policy was its retention of the mercantilism and protectionism of the old order. In this, the Republic led the way before the

Empire, even though it was under the Continental System of Napoleon that the demands of the French were pressed furthest. The idea of Napoleon as the good European was a twentieth-century myth, owing something to the desire of those who succumbed to it for an anticipation of the Nazi New Order which would give the latter some respectability. In fact, Napoleonic government, like that of the Convention and Directory, showed itself as exploitative, predatory, and protectionist as the old monarchy. Exploitation of the satellite economies by tariffs and prohibitions was merely a more respectable version of exploitation by levies in cash and kind, forced payment for services, and conscription.

Yet however others might see them—and Fanny Burney was startled on arriving in Calais in 1802 to discover that her husband's countrymen were not bloody monsters—the French saw themselves as liberators and their role outside France as a progressive and educative one. After 1815, moreover, many foreigners came to idealize them (or some of them) in this way; even some of those who had fought against them came round somewhat as the Restoration took hold. Those who had the most direct experience of French occupation did not, it is true, usually take this view, but a general impression that the French armies had somehow proved a liberating agency became current as the nineteenth century proceeded; this was, after all, how many conservatives had seen them and why they had fought against them.

In retrospect, French institutions certainly looked liberal in comparison with what had gone before. In the constitutions of the satellite republics of the Directory and the practice of the Napoleonic monarchs, equality before the law, the official end of feudal dues, the widening of the suffrage were usual, even if in practice this hardly added up to enough to offset a practical subordination to a French dictatorship. In the end, the fragility of these states and the fact that they collapsed so easily (in 1799 as well as in 1814) suggests that oppression and exploitation had produced a disillusion which outweighed any superficial liberalizing. Or, it may be, liberalizing was not what many people wanted, in any case. Evidently the Spanish people did not, for they turned on their own reformers for co-operating with the French.

The Spanish revolt which began in 1808 is revealing in another way. It was not only the most important peasant rising against the French and the biggest; it was also distinctive in a yet more important sense in being a national rising. Spain, of course, was already a nation in 1789 and did not need the French Revolution to tell it so; nonetheless, even in Spain an immense fillip was given to national feeling by the effort of the anti-French resistance. There is much to be said for the view that in so far as the French Revolution strengthened the idea of nationalism, it did so less by the positive promotion of the idea of popular sovereignty (important though that was to be to middle-class intellectuals) then by awakening a sense of community among the oppressed, or reinvigorating it where it already existed.

Certainly nationalism and nationality were central ideas of the political world after 1815 as they had never been before. The revolutions of the next century and more all over the world were to show their importance; many more men rose against their rulers in the cause of nationalism in the next hundred years than in that of socialist ideals (though it was sometimes held that the two were connected). Revolutionary or potentially revolutionary movements were increasingly thought to be legitimate if people recognized in them the cause of nationality. Another, less direct, expression of the new importance of the national idea was the general change which overtook the traditional view of the State in almost every European country except Russia during the next century. From being the organization by which rulers defended themselves against their subjects, the State became the expression and possession of the people—in theory at least. Much of the story of successful nation-building in nineteenth-century Europe was to be one of intelligent conservatives allying with the new legitimizing creed of nationality in order to retain their position. The process has come so far that it is very hard to think in our own day of a State being rightfully constituted unless it is theoretically the expression of a national will and the institutional embodiment of a nationality.

This was a real advance for Europe down a road very few nations had taken before 1789. So was the generalizing over a large area of the institutions of the market economy, even though their impact was usually even slower in making itself apparent than in France. The clearest and most visible result was in the countryside. Over most of western Germany either the direct operation of French law or the stimulus offered to change by the need to compete with France (as in the Prussian example) had significantly diminished the area of Europe over which seigneurial lordship and communal usage were dominant. The positive promotion of freer trade, it was true, had less success than the destruction of past forms, for the preservation of independent states with their own customs systems in both Germany and Italy was an effective check on the establishment of national markets.

Nationalism was a political idea, one component of a new kind of politics which was generalized Europe-wide by the French Revolution. The polarized model of politics, the notion that all political struggles are essentially a matter of specific and local embodiments of a permanently two-sided conflict between two irreconcilables—black versus white, progress versus reaction, Left versus Right—was another part of it. In seeking to explain the appeal of this idea, it is tempting to observe that there 'always' have been conflicts of temperaments and outlook which look like this: some people are usually happy with change, some unhappy; some are cautious, some bold; some like to innovate, some to consolidate. This, though, besides being easily recognizable as speculative psychology, gives no clue about what people may be expected to do in different circumstances. As a result of the Revolution men began to believe that all political questions, regardless of circumstantial differences, could be read as versions of the same fundamental conflict. All particular issues could be linked so as to divide men in a way which was always recognizable as expressions of two enduring ideological standpoints.

This idea may well be reckoned the Revolution's most influential legacy. It was to prove so successful in diffusing itself that in the twentieth century men have tried to apply it in practically every country in the world, even though in most of them the institutions and traditions making sense of it have only been experienced fitfully and superficially, if at all. The setting of new categories for politics which were to go round the world, coupled with the stimulus given to nationalism, was a great creative political achievement. Its practical results can best be discerned in the reorganization of Europe in the next century on the basis of nationality and the acceptance of this as legitimate, in the spread of liberalism in the vague (but easily recognizable) sense of the promotion of the liberation of the individual from restraints laid on him by tradition and authority, and in the acceptance by liberals and conservatives alike of the belief that the essential political issues of nineteenth-century Europe could be defined by attitudes towards a revolutionary cause whose content had been announced in 1789–94. Whether such a view led to optimism or pessimism is entirely irrelevant; it came to be held almost universally in continental Europe and even by some people in England. It was quite new. No one had thought about politics in this way before.

A new international structure

Older issues were not quite lost to sight in the pursuit of ideological aims and economic exploitation by the governments of France. In the narrower sense of foreign policy, the management of French power in relation to possible rivals, they often showed much continuity with the old order. One great book was once written to show that the key to French foreign policy from 1789 to 1815 was a quest to give France natural frontiers which had begun under Louis XIV. This no longer seems acceptable. It is clear, though, that the old open rivalry of Bourbon and Habsburg, glozed over by the reversal of alliances in the 1750s and the Austrian marriage, had reasserted itself by 1792; the declaration of war was not entirely to be understood in the context of the Revolution and its defence. In the next seventeen years, Austria was four times forced to terms, humbled by French arms; in the end she proved unable to hold off her old opponent without

Russian support. Four major peace treaties, those of Campo-Formio, Lunéville, Pressburg, and Schönbrunn, marked retreats of Habsburg power. The dissolution of the Holy Roman Empire and the marriage of Napoleon to an Austrian princess were spectacular registrations of dynastic if not of strategic and territorial decline. In the end, Austria emerged on the winning side only by admitting to the heart of Europe her great eastern rival, Russia. Austrian power in 1815 was more apparent than real, owing more to skilled diplomacy, Prussian modesty, and the retirement of Russian power once more to the East, than to her own resources. Nevertheless, she was perhaps better placed territorially than in 1792, for the encumbrance of the Austrian Netherlands had gone and she had made large gains of territory in Italy; nor in Germany did she suffer much by the disappearance of the ambiguous advantage of the old imperial tital. There was still to be one more Austro-French round, in fact, before the Habsburgs met at the hands of Prussia the defeat which finally reconciled them to limitation to a Danubian and south-eastern role.

The other rivalry inherited from the old order had been that with England. Here again, the governments of the Revolution reverted to an older pattern. When war was declared in 1793 on 'the new Carthage' as the French liked to call their old opponent, that was the end of the possibilities of *détente* inherent in the commercial treaty of 1786 (not that they had appealed to many Frenchmen). But France was without advantages she had enjoyed in the American war, and command of the sea meant that though the British could do virtually nothing on the continent without allies, they could have their way with French commerce and colonies. In fact, the British soon saw much more in the struggle than this. Both the ruling class and an appreciable sector of what was beginning to be called 'public opinion' quickly envisaged the war as a national and an ideological struggle. Significantly, the British never gave up referring to Napoleon as 'General Bonaparte'; they saw themselves as fighting the same enemy, the Revolution, throughout, and Napoleon only as its latest agent. His ambitions and efforts to satisfy them did much to justify their view. On both sides, the Anglo-French struggle brought into play real popular animosities and passions. In England, too, this led to some modification of her own politics, which began to take on a more ideological colour.

The outcome of the Anglo-French struggle was another British victory registered in the traditional way, outside Europe. The French strategy of subversion failed because it could not be brought to bear with the support of French arms in Ireland. The alternative of economic warfare incurred diplomatic costs for France in quarrels with other states which in the end proved too great. The British strategy of keeping alive resistance in Europe was well-suited to the war's strategic shape, while its other prong, the assertion of maritime supremacy, succeeded brilliantly and left in British hands at the peace virtually all of the French colonial empire which had still been retained by France after the Seven Years' War. This was not without heavy cost. Great Britain took a long time after 1815 to resume the attitude of unconcern about the European balance of power which had been urged on her traditionally by the 'blue-water' school.

The Revolution outside Europe

The Anglo-French contest itself suggests—correctly—that Europe is not the whole story of the Revolution abroad. Though the Revolution's impact was not everywhere the same, it was worldwide. Objectively, often blindly, the repercussions of French policy changed the fates of lands far away; this could be of enormous significance. The Louisiana Purchase was a by-product of the strategic and diplomatic exigences Napoleon faced in Europe, but it immediately doubled the territorial extent of the United States, and it assured the young republic a continental future. Subjectively, the Revolution had other effects, too; it could awake imitation and inspire new sorts of politics through its example and mythology.

This is perhaps observable first in the Caribbean, where there was an important French presence in 1789. In the plantation colony of San Domingo, the western end of Hispaniola, or Haiti as it is now called, there were something like 40,000 Frenchmen. There were also about a half-million blacks, the overwhelming majority of them slaves, and many persons of mixed blood. Their relationship with one another were bound to be deeply affected both by the law and policy of the metropolitan government and by the revolutionary example. Many Frenchmen in France were interested in the fate of the island, too, whether through their connections with Caribbean trade and investment, or through the lucrative slave trade in which Nantes played the major part and which was at its height in the 1780s.

The first to seek to utilize the implications of the principles of 1789 were the planters, who sought and obtained representation in the National Assembly. But the 'friends of the blacks' (*Amis des Noirs*) who had even before the Revolution been advocating the abolition of slavery brought it into the political arena and at once met determined opposition from the colonists' lobby. The free blacks and mulattoes had their own case to make, too; they might not want to end slavery (some of them were slave-owners), but they sought to share the rights of other French citizens.

The Constituent first admitted all duly qualified persons living in the colonies, white or black, to citizenship, but this provoked furious outcry from the white planters. This was the beginning of deepening disorder, complicated successively by the coming of the war (which involved the Spanish authorities in the eastern end of the island) and by internal politics in France as white colonists swung round to royalism. The Constituent in the end had given way to them and just before it left power had left the question of black citizenship in their hands. This produced negro rebellion. The Convention then accorded blacks full citizenship and thus drove the whites into counter-revolution. Soon there was a civil war between two white parties, with continuing black revolt as its background. Then, in 1794, the Convention abolished slavery in the French colonies; not all of them applied the decree but in San Domingo this rallied the black leaders and briefly restored order to the island. Under the effective rule of one outstanding black man, Toussaint l'Ouverture, the island (the whole of which had nominally passed under French rule after the peace with Spain) was fairly peaceful until the Consulate. Two fatal steps were then taken: the re-establishment of slavery by law in the French colonies and the dispatch of a French army to reduce San Domingo. The attempt was unsuccessful; though l'Ouverture was carried off to France, the French army was destroyed, and more ferocious massacres than any yet seen in the island accompanied the inauguration in 1804 of the first black republic set up anywhere in the world. This was Haiti. It was to have an unhappy history (and was almost at once thrown into a new period of turmoil by a tyrant who proclaimed himself emperor), but this does not diminish the interest of its emergence. It was there both because the Revolution had disrupted the old order and because the revolutionary example was so powerful that even a black community still relatively close to its African roots turned not to its traditional institution but to those of French republicanism when it sought to stabilize its new-born independence.

To other new American nations, other European traditions contributed more, yet for all the importance of the Spanish and Portuguese legacies, the influence of the Revolution was paramount in determining much of the process and something of the tone of politics in the republics which emerged in Central and South America in the early nineteenth century. Once again, the Revolution's influence was felt both objectively and subjectively. The effective separation of the Spanish colonies from the metropolis which followed a French invasion of Spain in 1808 provided a fruitful experience of self-direction for the colonial élites. This crystallized the consequences of long-sensed practical irritations and ideological stimuli. To the latter, though, France may be reckoned to have added her own contribution from the 1790s, when the Venezuelan Miranda arrived in Paris to seek help against Spanish colonial rule (he subsequently served, not altogether successfully, with the French army in Belgium). Yet Miranda, inspired by the American War of Independence against the British, had been committed to the anti-imperialist cause before the French Revolution. It seems, in fact, that the most important French revolutionary influence in South America

was through the objective conditions for liberation which it
favoured by assuring them *de facto* independence of Spanish
rule. After *de jure* independence, the story changed. Then the
conditions of South American politics and the cultural orientation of its élites gave their political forms and programmes
a vocabulary and frame of reference which strongly reflected
the European world of post-revolutionary politics, and therefore the influence of the Revolution at one remove.

Within the Ottoman empire, too, there were some immediately visible repercussions. Among the Christian populations
of the empire—notably the Armenians and the inhabitants
of the Greek peninsula—the ideals of the Revolution left traces
on nationalist movements. But such movements had in some
cases anticipated 1789 and, again, the objective impact of
events provoked by the Revolution seems more immediately
important. In this instance, it can be dated precisely, to 1798,
the year when the Directory sent an expedition under Bonaparte to Egypt. This opened the story of nation-making in
the Islamic lands of the Ottoman empire. After this blow at
Ottoman authority a virtually independent Egypt, subject to
the Sultan in name only and ruled by Mehemet Ali,
emerged within a few years.

In Asia, the story is harder to seize but even there something can be sensed. The thought that Tippoo Sahib might
succeed in obtaining the French support held out to him led
the British to overthrow him—this might be reckoned the
most remote of the objective consequences of the Revolution
(though years later the British were still worrying about a
French invasion of the Indus valley with much less reason).
Further east still, in Indonesia and Japan, ripples of the
ideological impact of the Revolution have been detected,
though later than in India; Muslim pilgrims from Java to
Mecca, it seems, travelling on to Turkey, picked up there
stories of what had happened in Europe; while one of the
Japanese who sought in the 1870s to give a democratic twist
to the Meiji Restoration explicitly used the French Revolution as an inspiration. With such remote responses, though,
the influence of the Revolution dissolves into its legacy to
political mythology, a legacy still at work today.

6

The Revolution as history and myth

IT will already be evident that the Revolution is in one sense the creation of historians. In addition, it is a creation which is constantly being remade. Of course, this is not all there is to be said about its nature nor for all purposes the most important, but it is important nonetheless. Questions about its beginning and origins, its duration and end, have always included implicit or explicit demands for statements about what the Revolution was and what it meant. Some of these demands and the answers they have called forth have become historical forces in their own right. In this way historical views about the Revolution demand our attention.

Some participants in the Revolution began to set out their answers at a very early date. The theory that there must have been someone to blame, that it was all the result of plots, for example, appealed to many people and they urged it on their contemporaries. Some blamed individuals: the duke of Orléans was much attacked by royalists who thought he was stirring up trouble in order to usurp the Crown, and it was not long before anglophobes began to detect the influence of 'Pitt's gold' in what was going on. Others identified groups as the miscreants: Protestants were among the first to be accused of subversion, the formulation of charges against them beginning in 1787 when attempts were made to muster Catholic opinion against the Crown's easing of some of their worst legal and civil disabilities. At different times, Jews, freemasons, and *philosophes* were all blamed for the Revolution and sometimes the roots of their supposed plots were traced very far back, to such implausible sources as the order of Knights Templar, or the Manichean heretics of the fourth century.

However wild, such ideas reveal something about the Revolution. This was the immensity of the psychological and emotional impression it made. It was an event—or series of events—which so struck many thinking men that it seemed to require a quite extraordinary and unusual explanation. Their culture lacked both our relativism and the taste for determinist explanations now taken for granted throughout much of the world of European tradition. It was also one which was soaked in assumptions of human responsibility. The notion of an eternal struggle of good and evil which lay at the heart of the Christian tradition was bound to make men look at first for historical explanations in terms of human volition. Such a bias was not reserved to the opponents of the Revolution; Barnave, a revolutionary politician who was possibly the first man to analyse the Revolution in terms of historical materialism, believed nevertheless that the property relations which he thought were fundamental to social change expressed themselves in action as the demands of specific groups; these could be deflected or inflamed by the wisdom or folly of rulers and leaders. Other admirers of the Revolution looked back and saw it as the culmination of enlightened thought or of a democratic movement whose origins lay in the French communes of the Middle Ages. Even before 1789, some of them had encouraged men to look forward to a great liberation which would in some sense sum up the past trends in human development, celebrating the work done by the *philosophes* and earlier reformers in preparing the way for what was to come.

For all that, the most impressive of the early attempts to generalize explanations of the French Revolution in terms of will were hostile. The first and most successful was Edmund Burke's, published in 1790 with the title *Reflections on the Revolution in France* and soon enjoying reprinting and translation in many countries. Burke did not spend much time on specific villains, or even on specific groups of villains, though he was happy to denounce the members of the National Assembly as the 'calculators and sophisters' characteristic of a new age *en passant*. But his target was in fact a very old and general one: human pride and presumption. He saw in the Revolution an outstanding example of the original sin of an inherently feeble and misleading instrument, the human intellect in which many of the thinkers of his day had mistakenly placed their faith. Burke could not believe that it was prudent to follow abstract argument and human desire in the management of society, when such guidance as was provided by the scrutiny of historic institutions, or of national history, of customs and habits and, above all, of religion, were available. To reject such guidance was wilful imprudence; good could not come of it.

Put like this, stripped of his magnificent rhythms and imagery, Burke's message does not now seem very striking and, to a secular age, it is perhaps merely curious. Yet it was of the first importance and remains one of the outstanding achievements of British political and social thought. This is not merely because the development of events soon seemed to confirm Burke's warnings all too well. It certainly helped, and drew the admiration of contemporaries to the book, that Frenchmen so soon abandoned the liberal tolerance they sought to show at the outbreak of the Revolution and turned to killing one another. In this way, the grave consequences of the self-assertiveness Burke had diagnosed seemed amply apparent three or four years after he wrote. What was more important was that he grasped the scale and import of events in France at a time when most Europeans still saw them as primarily of merely domestic concern to Frenchmen, of interest to foreign governments only because they might affect relations between states. Burke, before anyone else, gave the Revolution its full weight as an event in the history of civilization. He was able to do this because of his deep sense of historical reality, of the continuity of the social fabric in time, and of the rooting of moral and political principles in the circumstances of national cultures.

In this sense, Burke may be said to have founded the historical interpretation of the Revolution by being the first who strove to assess its universal significance: others of his day and generation might emphasize it as a moment in a single process—whether for good or ill—and therefore linked to the past, but Burke's argument put the question on a different plane by emphasizing that what was changing was more than a matter of a few reforms; it was the whole basis of civilization as men knew it. This, in principle, involved every aspect of society. He was not, of course, the only thinker of the time to contribute to a new sense of society and community as an organic growth. Rousseau (whose ideas he despised and hated, for all they had in common with his own) had already said much which can be read in this sense, and Herder drew on a range of linguistic and anthropological evidence which Burke did not employ. But his orientation of thought towards history was the greatest single step in the early understanding of the Revolution. Above all, since it anchored the Revolution in a historical and therefore an evolving process, it was to make possible a conservative inter- pretation of the Revolution on another basis than that of the dogmatic moral and theological absolutism of those in con- tinental Europe who followed the Savoyard intellectual, De Maistre.

The sense that the Revolution was an event in the history of mankind whose explanation was to be sought historically had deep and lasting effects. It also raised grave difficulties, among them some already noticed, in the definition of its extent and the selection of significant data. It is an exaggeration, but one bearing in the right direction, to say that Hegel's whole philosophy of history was a response to grappling with these problems. Hegel sought to seize the Revolution's importance as a moment in the evolution of the human mind and to explain the extraordinary paradox it demonstrated that progressive movement might be unavoid- ably and irreparably combined with violent spasms of retro- gression, conflict, confusion. His particular concerns did not require him to define precisely his chronological conception of the Revolution (though he seems to have thought that it ought to encompass the Napoleonic era) and many other writers who tried to approach it in terms of transcendent or immanent historical processes found it equally difficult to do so. Writing in the late 1830s, Carlyle could still observe that the Revolution, the greatest event of the age, was not yet over. Marx, materializing the process Hegel had discerned into a matter of changes in the relations between classes (and picking up ideas he had found in the literature of the revolutionary era itself), seems to have thought it unnecessary to define with dates what he meant by the French Revolution, though he remarked a special importance in the years 1793–5.

The political use of the Revolution

It is nonetheless broadly true to say that the medium through which the Revolution was refracted and through which images of it formed and dissolved in the nineteenth century tended to concentrate attention upon the events of 1789 to 1799 and even to emphasize especially the first half of that decade. This medium was the political rhetoric of the age. In France the events of 1830 and 1848, and the disaster of the Paris Commune of 1871, all led to evocation, celebration, and retrospective condemnation of the resounding days of the Great Revolution. Tocqueville and Marx both thought that the men of 1848 were actually mimicking—whether consciously or unconsciously—the gestures, language, and behaviour of the revolutionaries half-a-century earlier who were depicted in so many popular prints. The journals of the Second Republic revived and evoked the titles of famous periodicals of the 1790s—*L'Ami du Peuple, Le nouveau père Duchesne*—and the slogan 'Liberty, Equality, Fraternity' was revived to gain a currency it had never enjoyed until then. It even became the official motto of the new state.

The events of the Commune showed how deep this mythological revivalism could go on both sides of the chasm which was felt to divide French society. 'Their memory is always with me' (*leur souvenir m'est toujours présent*) said one of the Communard leaders of 1871 of the men of the Convention, whom he saw in a far simpler light than historians now allow us to do. The very word 'Commune' evoked glorious or infamous memories according to your judgement of the 'insurrectionary Commune' of Paris which had appeared in 1792 and had actually organized the rising which ended the monarchy, or of the Commune of the Year III, dominated by the henchmen of Robespierre. Sometimes the parallels were very close indeed: as late as 1880, a monarchist senator could oppose the adoption of 14 July as a national holiday and urge upon his listeners the similarity between the lynchings which had followed the fall of the Bastille and those which had detonated the Commune more than eighty years later.

Politicians were in the first place haunted by the revolutionary past because of the power its images gave them to move themselves and others. But they also drew from it categories in which to think. These often pinned down their ideas in cramping ways. One result was a habit of drawing inferences about what was likely to happen. This only reached its extreme and most paranoiac form in the haunting obsession of some Bolsheviks (Trotsky among them) with the danger of 'Thermidor', the ending of a 'democratic' phase of the Revolution, or with the emergence of a soldier—a 'Bonaparte' —who would capture it. (The men of 1789, brooding on this danger, had feared a 'Cromwell', which ought, perhaps, to have suggested to later observers that the Revolution did not invent *de novo* the whole of politics.) In this way, too, alarmed conservatives feared a new Terror might follow anti-clerical manifestations under the early Third Republic, while radicals then denounced the tradition of 'Coblenz', the rallying-place for the emigrant princes in 1792.

Such ideas had some forcefulness in shaping the tradition of French historiography about the Revolution, which was rooted not in academic concern but in politics. There has rarely been a subject more politicized from the outset than the French Revolution. Sieyès' famous (and dully written) book, *Qu'est-ce-que le Tiers Etat?*, announced in 1789 themes which run through subsequent writings by identifying the Revolution with the triumph (he thought for good) of the property-owning non-noble middle class. It was the development and inversion of this theme of the Revolution as class struggle which enabled the Italian revolutionary Buonarroti later to interpret the fall of Robespierre and the subsequent failure of the social revolutionary Babeuf as confirmation of his thesis that a democratic revolution had been captured, dammed up, frozen or in some other way thwarted by the classes whose interests were preferred to those of the masses. Thus was formulated the core of Marx's view of the Revolution long before he wrote.

A political concern was also evident in the first and still the greatest historical analysis of the Revolution, Alexis de Tocqueville's *L'Ancien Régime*, published in 1856, under the Second Empire. This incomplete work surveys only the background from which the Revolution emerged; though a second volume was to have dealt with the events of the Revolution itself, only notes for it remained when Tocqueville died. The main lines of his overall interpretation of the Revolution are clear, nevertheless, and they were emphatically shaped by a political concern. Tocqueville wished to explain the roots of the situation he observed (and regretted) in his own day. He looked out on a France in which all attempts to establish a liberal political order since 1815 seemed to have failed, and a dictatorship had been established by force by Napoleon III. Throughout the rest of the western world too, he thought, the symptoms could be detected of an oncoming democratic— by which he meant egalitarian and antagonized—social order in which not only liberty but the values of civilized culture would be threatened.

Tocqueville's explanation why the Revolution had failed to establish the free society glimpsed by many of its promoters at the outset rested, in essence, on the brilliant assertion of a paradox: he argued that the Revolution had not broken with the old order, but confirmed its deepest tendencies, grew naturally and continuously out of them and, so far as it destroyed and innovated, did so at the cost of just those elements in the old order which had most obstructed the unrolling of its deepest tendencies. These were towards the centralization and reinforcement of the power of government, and the complementary process of reducing society to an aggregate of juridically equal, atomized individuals, each purged of the ties of locality, blood, and occupation which could distinguish him from others and might therefore strengthen his resistance to oppression and enrich his contribution to society and civilization.

Apart from Burke's, Tocqueville's book is the only intellec-

tual masterpiece to have been written about the Revolution
(one by Michelet is an artistic masterpiece, though), and like
its forerunner it was written with an intense concern and
political commitment. The temper of the two works is, nonetheless, very different: Burke declaims (nobly, movingly,
angrily, and sometimes piteously), carrying his readers along
by main force, where Tocqueville (coldly and sometimes
bitterly) analyses, delineates, and describes. Burke's book is
a sermon; Tocqueville's the first major piece of historical
sociology on the topic and one whose specific arguments have
still a remarkable impressiveness, even after detailed modern
scholarship has done its worst with them. (Indeed, they
perhaps look more impressive now than two or three decades
ago.) This impressiveness, nonetheless, is the product of a
commitment as unyielding as Burke's. Tocqueville's political
bias enabled him to treat the Revolution at a level which
transcended questions of the responsibilities of individuals and
parties. Partisan he was, nevertheless, his outlook being that
of a conservative libertarian.

Most nineteenth-century French writers on the Revolution
continued to be preoccupied instead with enquiry at a lower
level about the responsibilities of actors in the Revolution.
Interpretation progressed, in so far as it did progress, by
disputing, refining, or formulating judgements about individuals or their standpoints. Already before Tocqueville wrote,
the poet Lamartine had established himself as the first considerable writer to discriminate importantly among those
equally regarded with horror by conservatives as terrorists.
This he did in his *Histoire des Girondins*, published in 1847;
even Robespierre, their destroyer, received back-handed
respect as the apostle of an unreal Utopia of unimpeachable
republicanism. The reputation of Robespierre, it may be said,
provides something of a touchstone of the political use of the
Revolution even down to the present day. Emerging from
royalist caricature which presented him as a tyrannical and
blood-thirsty monster who personified the essential nature
of the Revolution, Robespierre's image has since undergone
a dazzling series of transformations. It has, nevertheless,
better kept its primacy as the supreme embodiment of the

essential nature of the Revolution among his admirers—who have now transformed him into a good, much misunderstood social reformer, thwarted by evil men—than among his detractors, who have gradually relegated him to the side of a stage dominated by more impersonal forces.

Yet even such a change as this embodies political decisions. Try as they might, Frenchmen found it impossible to shake politics out of revolutionary historiography. The climax of the political interpretation of the Revolution in fact came only after the establishment of the Third Republic. This change brought about the triumph of the pro-revolutionaries, who (with the agreement of their opponents) so successfully identified the Revolution with republicanism that the fathers of the new regime became custodians of the Revolution as a national possession. Under the Third Republic, the Revolution was integrated with the nation's traditional culture for the Left in a way as important and unquestioned as was the cause of religion identified with France on the Right. The centenary of 1789 was in due course impressively and officially celebrated; royalist demonstrations for the centenaries of the September Massacres, and of the execution of Louis XVI, had nothing like the same impact.

The scholarly study of the Revolution

There had always been a few who, from scholarly instinct or antiquarian passion, had studied the Revolution like any other great event as a subject for erudition and criticism. Under the Third Republic the scholarly study of the Revolution at last became institutionalized and the foundations of modern academic methods were laid. Journals of the history of the Revolution began to appear which, from somewhat feeble intellectual seedlings, grew into major scholarly publications. It was of the first importance that in 1885 a chair of the history of the Revolution was created at the Sorbonne, thanks to the radically inclined city council of Paris. With its occupation by Alphonse Aulard, greatest of the pre-1914 generation of republican historians, the subject-matter of Revolutionary history passed at last from its antiquarian to its scholarly phase. Yet this was far from meaning that ideology was left outside the lecture-room. In a series of lectures, articles, and books, Aulard expounded the theme—grateful to the ears of the middle-of-the-road parliamentarians of the Third Republic—that the essential nature of the Revolution was the impulse towards the establishment of the Republic as the guardian of the ideals of liberty and civic equality. France was, in this view, indisputably a democracy, but a political and social democracy, not an economic one, having faced (and faced down) the challenge of socialism in the Revolution itself.

Broadly speaking—and no more can be attempted in so brief a book as this—the ideological history of French Revolutionary studies in France since the beginning of this century has been the successful challenging of such ideas as these by interpretations drawn from further Left along the historical spectrum. The sources of this challenge have been manifold. In part, it rests on a rediscovery or reassertion of things said long ago, of the development of ideas whose roots lie in the Babeuf episode, for example. In part it lies in personal animus and predilection. But its overwhelmingly most important source has been the diffusion of a broadly Marxist interpretation—the French have the useful word *marxisant*, which is easier to say than 'Marx-ish' would be—which asserts that the Revolution's 'meaning' was that it represented the achievement of power in France by the class Marx had identified as the *bourgeoisie* (the owners of industrial and commercial capital). To this was usually added an indulgence of a sense of righteous indignation about what had followed this promising beginning. Not for the first or last time, sociological determinism was riveted to moral disapproval to provide a viewpoint which enabled its exponents to be at one and the same time sniffy about the men who had triumphed in the Revolution (or were presumed to have done so) and exultant about the objective and unequivocally progressive significance of what they were supposed to have done.

The most important landmark in the development of this point of view was the *Histoire socialiste de la révolution française* edited by the great French socialist politician, Jean Jaurès. It began to appear in 1901. Though uneven, it remains a fine work and a useful one, stimulating in its sweep and panoramic view and directing attention to social history in quite a new way. It was to be of seminal importance, too, in inspiring much of the work of the most important and influential of all twentieth-century scholars of the Revolution, Georges Lefebvre.

Nevertheless, Lefebvre's importance was for years obscured somewhat by the productivity and violence of another French scholar, Albert Mathiez, whose standpoint on many matters was not dissimilar to his, but who had a less unhurried approach to publication than Lefebvre and showed much more personal animus against his critics. For the first two decades of this century, the din and smoke of a continuous attack by Mathiez on Aulard distracted attention from more important issues. From a political position leftish rather than consistently Marxist (though he was for a time a member of the French Communist party in the 1920s), Mathiez conducted a vendetta rather than a debate. His chosen ground was a quarrel about Robespierre, who became for him an immaculate figure; conversely, Mathiez poured vilification on Danton, whom Aulard had praised as the defender of popular republicanism. The result was a prolonged and valuable fall-out of detailed information about two political biographies (badly overdue in Robespierre's case) and a new appreciation of Robespierre's stature. Much re-thinking was also stimulated about the divisions which separated men in the Convention. But for all Mathiez's commitment to a generalized belief that the poor had done less well out of the Revolution than they were entitled to and the sensitivity to social issues he evinced in a major book and a huge corpus of reviews and critical comments, his scholarship had a predominantly political focus. This somewhat masked the importance of the way ahead to which Jaurès' work pointed and delayed its exploitation.

This in the end had its fruition in the work of Lefebvre. Directed to the central themes of French social history, it changed thinking about the Revolution more than that of any other single scholar in this century. Above all in his studies of rural France, Lefebvre opened new areas of investigation which have already yielded a huge enrichment of knowledge, much of which has made old generalizations and simplifications untenable. Yet, for all this, Lefebvre's overall view of the Revolution was uncompromisingly clear and Marxist: he described a revolution of the *bourgeoisie*, and, moreover, a bourgeois revolution on a worldwide stage and not merely a French one. Substantially, this remains prevailing French orthodoxy in these matters, expressed in its most cut-and-dried form in some of the more general statements and books of Professor Albert Soboul. The heart of this orthodoxy is the old assertion that in the Revolution the French *bourgeoisie* seized power and used it to restructure society and economy alike in their own interests.

Curiously, this overall interpretation remains authoritative even though much of the detailed work of French scholars—among whom must be numbered Lefebvre and Soboul—suggests it is inadequate. The heart of the matter is that the analytical categories of the established Marxist view have increasingly been shown to be crude and anachronistic. Of all of them, none is more misleading than '*bourgeoisie*', and none seems less appropriate as a label for the men who made the Revolution, if we are to take that term in the Marxist sense of the possessors of industrial and commercial capital. Certainly the pattern of events in 1789 is not reducible to a struggle of '*bourgeois*' and non-capitalist noblemen. Nor is there to be found any socio-economic group before the Revolution resembling, say, the English manufacturing interest of the following century. It is not unfair to say that the *bien-pensants* of Marxist orthodoxy have given scant weight to these objections, contenting themselves, by and large, with the reiteration of the well-known fact that France gave itself in the Revolution institutions which ought to have favoured the transition to capitalism from feudalism.

English and American scholars have found it easier to grapple with such considerations than have the French. This may well owe less to their ideological formation (whatever it may be) than a long tradition of Anglo-Saxon scholarship and interest in the French Revolution whose roots lie in the great conflict with revolutionary France. This led to the formulation at an early date of stereotypes which long resisted demolition and erosion. In the United States they shaped party division in the young republic. In England there was an unwillingness to discriminate among Frenchmen, especially after Bonaparte had established himself. Yet the first great foreign narrative of the Revolution was British. This was Carlyle's *French Revolution*, published in 1837, just between two periods of political upheaval during which the meaning and implication of what had happened in France were much invoked by English publicists and politicians. Carlyle was himself deeply aware of the interconnection of events of his own day with the events in France forty years earlier. His sources were for the most part memoirs which gave a political emphasis to his narrative. Yet he wrote about more than politics, and his book is now as unjustly neglected as it was once outstandingly popular. Though the outline of the scenario it presents is simple enough, the book is of great complexity; there are few outright villains and the texture of social life is vividly evoked. In this complexity, the predominant impression is of violence; this side of the Revolution has never been so skilfully portrayed in English. The people—the crowd in Paris and the peasants of the countryside—were brought by Carlyle into the English historical consciousness of the Revolution as more than a vague uproar in the background.

Through him, too, they reached a wide public. They lived again, moreover, in another work which was based on his own and was even more influential in diffusing a particular interpretation of the Revolution, Dickens' novel *A Tale of Two Cities*, published in 1859. Through this conduit the interpretation of the Revolution as above all a popular upheaval was to reach even larger audiences. More blatantly and crudely didactic than Carlyle, and more black-and-white in his judgements, Dickens preached a simple and traditional moral message: as a man sows, so shall he reap. Nonetheless, he concentrated attention remarkably upon the people. It is the Faubourg St. Antoine and the country estate which provide settings for his revolutionaries, not the revolutionary assemblies; there is no politician drawn from life in its pages (such as, for example, the pathetic Lord George Gordon of *Barnaby Rudge*). Interestingly, Dickens also anticipated in one respect the conclusions of much modern scholarship in that he identified the programme of his violent revolutionaries not as one of precisely formulated goals, but as a generalized social ideal, the maintenance of a certain sense of justice and a traditional moral code.

It was a long time before English scholarship was to reflect such themes. During the nineteenth century, those engaged in the academic study of the Revolution directed their attention more to the rising tide of political memoir and monograph. For all his moralizing about individual rectitude, the lectures which Acton gave at Cambridge in the 1890s and published in 1910 are perhaps the finest memorial of this phase. Acton began with two convictions which told in the same direction. The first was that one of the central concerns of the historian should be the explanation of his own times (to which the Revolution had contributed so much) and that this confirmed a general reading of history as the story of liberty. The second was that historical techniques had at last reached the point at which definitive answers could be given to all questions on which full documentation was available. 'In a few years', he once rashly observed of the Revolution, 'all that can be known will be known.' It is a tribute to Acton's intellectual quality that he should still be worth reading now that his assumptions have crumbled.

Acton's view of the Revolution was almost entirely dominated by politics and, for that matter, by the politics which went on in the Assemblies and the Jacobin club of Paris. In this, he merely reflected the bias of the documentation and the state of up-to-date French scholarship at the end of the century. He explored this limited area with great intellectual acuteness, but a slight mustiness, a faintly academic smell, lingers over his writing, for all his own passion about the topics he discussed. At home as he was with the great European political issues of his own day and with the culture of other countries, Acton was further from emotional involvement in the social and emotional battles of the Revolution than was Carlyle. His distress, even horror, over Bacourt's revelation that Mirabeau was much like any other politician and his pursed-lips verdict on the Girondins do not show much sense of the pressures and currents in which revolutionary politicians moved. Yet, it must be repeated, he is still worth reading not only because he was a man of distinguished intellect, but because his enormous and detailed learning enabled him to provide constant reminders of the importance in the Revolution of the contingent and circumstantial. In this respect at least he was an important antidote to ideological interpretation.

In the first half of the twentieth century, the most influential English historian of the Revolution was J. M. Thompson. Not himself what is now called a 'researcher' in the archives, he made available to a large public the conclusions and consequent re-interpretations which were emerging from French scholarship, and brought them before a numerous body of pupils. This was a most important service. His books show a distance and detachment from the subject which some have found too cool; yet the catholicity of Thompson's sympathies gave a much greater humanity to his writing than Acton's shows. In one respect, too, he confirmed (as was natural, for it dominated French historiography at that time) a chronological narrowness of approach. Thompson's Revolution began in 1789 and ended in 1794, with Robespierre's downfall. Neither pre-Revolution nor post-Thermidor much interested him. Nor did he strive to assess the wider implications of the Revolution, its international, cultural significance.

Since Thompson's day and often because of the work of his pupils, much more notice has been taken by the French of English writing on the history of the French Revolution. This has largely been dominated by the work of two men of very different approach and temperament, the late Alfred Cobban and Professor Richard Cobb. Both have made the French take them seriously—never an easy thing for an English scholar to achieve in this field—and both have by their work altered the shape of the historical landscape. Cobban's major achievement was critical rather than exploratory. In a series of lectures published in 1964 he drew attention to unresolved contradictions, weaknesses in chains of argument and unsupported assertions which were bound up in the quasi-Marxist French orthodoxy. Professor Cobb has proceeded differently, by burrowing down into the detailed and personal experience of the Revolution in its best-documented years (those from 1793 onwards). He has broken up a surface skated over in many elegant variations of the generalizations based on the politics of Paris; for millions of Frenchmen, he has pointed out in a memorable phrase, the Revolution was a 'magnificent irrelevance' and at some moments his work has appeared almost to be about to dissolve the Revolution altogether into a continuum of low life spanning the old order and nineteenth-century France. Yet his work has been in its effect not totally unlike that of Cobban. Both of them forced on their pupils and their critics an almost total reconsideration of the most elementary forms and categories within which were set earlier views of the Revolution.

Meanwhile, American twentieth-century scholarship, for a long time dominated by Leo Gershoy, who wrote broadly within the parameters set by the Mathiez-Lefebvre generation, has also begun to question old categories. Besides a great deal of important work on specific topics, now embodied in monographs, general ideas underwent reconsideration, one of the most striking of their manifestations being the appearance of a large two-volume book in which Professor R. R. Palmer surveyed world political changes in the later eighteenth century and concluded that the French Revolution had to be embodied in a 'democratic' revolutionary movement apparent in almost every country in Europe and in North America, if it was to be understood aright. An idea similar, but not quite identical with this was also taken up in France, where there was some interest in what was called an 'Atlantic Revolution'. These large adumbrations did not prove easy to defend against precise and detailed criticism; the categories to which data drawn from different countries were assimilated were sometimes anachronistic, often mis-leadingly over-simplified, and very different general inter-pretations might be placed on the histories of individual countries in the Revolutionary era. In the end attempts to absorb the French Revolution into a wave of 'democratic' revolution have proved damp squibs. Nevertheless, they had some value in directing attention away from the internal development of the Revolution and towards assessment of its international significance—something which had hitherto tended to be reduced to such simple and misleading propositions as that France 'led' the age towards liberty and the triumph of capitalism.

The present scene

In assessing the present state of scholarly interest in the Revolution, it is necessary to set aside at the outset consideration of the valuable work often being done within well-established guidelines, for there is not time to deal with everything. The orthodox French tradition continues to produce excellent specific studies; often, too, they fit comfortably into the frameworks of publication provided by old-established journals and such series as the volumes published by the *Commission d'histoire économique et sociale de la Révolution française* set up before the Great War. It is also important not to be over-impressed by the volume of publication occasioned in certain narrow fields, where new material and a new ideological enthusiasm have resulted in an increase of published material and a new intensification of detailed knowledge without disclosing much of general interest; the outstanding example is the Franco-Italian-Russian Babeuf/Buonarroti industry. By way of balance, though, due recognition must be given to the fact that only the mining of certain seams of long-established scholarship to the point at which they return very little has revealed that new approaches are needed. We should all be the historically poorer without Mathiez's vast work on the personal politics of the *conventionnel* leaders. Only what he did made it necessary to turn elsewhere.

One obvious large-scale development is a major re-orientation of social history around statistical data. This is a development to which Lefebvre showed the way in his work on peasant history, but which has now been carried back into the eighteenth and forward into the nineteenth century. Among other effects, it stimulated scholars long dissatisfied with chopping off the history of the Revolution at arbitrary dates. It has also revivified local history. The later years of the nineteenth century and the first of our own produced a flood of local studies, but these were often merely hagiographical or antiquarian, recalling the glories of epic struggles of priest and local Jacobin club, or the battles of patriot and royalist, thus projecting backwards into history the political quarrels of the Third Republic. This has now given way to an era of systematic local and regional study of major themes. The bearing of these, it is now clear, is hard to grasp at the level of national government unless their operation locally and in detail is understood: food-supply and the working of the *Maximum*; 'de-Christianization' and resistance to juror priests intruded from outside; the realities of the personal and traditional feuds fought out within the framework provided by Revolutionary government. Such local studies owe much to the encouragement and example of Lefebvre, whose own doctoral thesis (published as long ago as 1924) remains one of the finest and most monumental among them: *Les paysans du Nord pendant la Révolution*.

Even such books do not tell the whole story of expansion and illumination in social history, which is possibly the single area of Revolution studies to profit most from new approaches. Orthodoxy here also has recently been challenged by the breaking-down of the simple, mechanistic arguments and categories into which Marxist interpretation always tended to fall. There has been a revelation of the complexity of social tissue; the Revolution now looked more like a stew in which different elements swirl about, than a layer-cake of clearly distinguishable strata. Paradoxically, one of the most important of all contributions to this tendency has come from two scholars who specifically identify themselves as Marxist, the Englishman George Rudé and the Frenchman Soboul. The former's book on *The Crowd in the French Revolution* and the latter's magnificent thesis *Les sansculottes parisiens en l'an II* made it possible to explain the Parisian 'popular movement'

(a phrase itself in danger of hardening into a mere argu-
mentative counter) and showed, too, its incomprehensibility
within categories derived from the class structures of developed
capitalism.

Another recent enrichment of Revolutionary historiography has been its extension into the realms of mentality
and the new complexities revealed there. There has long
been an interest in the contribution of ideas to the events of
the Revolution. There has been an assumption that the ideas
of the Enlightenment had, somehow, a special responsibility
for what happened after 1789 which has always been taken
for granted by the mythologists of Left and Right alike, and
this has been expressed in many studies tracing the lineage
of such ideas back to Locke or even further. Recently,
though, something more than this has been attempted in the
study of ideas, and attempted very fruitfully. This is the
recovery of the states of minds, conscious and unconscious
assumptions, attitudes, prejudices, and emotions of large
numbers of men. Enquiry has been pressed forwards on these
topics in many ways. Some historians have chosen to scrutinize
institutions such as the pious fraternities of the old order,
masonic lodges, or the Revolutionary festivals which replaced
the holidays of the old Christian calendar, seeing them as
means by which mentality expressed itself in behaviour.
Others have turned to language; that of the *cahiers*, for
instance, or that of Revolutionary orators. The responses
evoked by the events of the religious struggles of the Revolution are another large body of material for such studies—
deliberate desecration associated with 'de-Christianization',
the struggles in communities between the adherents of rival
priests, for example.

Overall, one of the most striking facts about almost all
recent studies, whether of mentality, society, or the economy,
is that they point in a direction already remarked ten years
or so ago, and now more evident than ever in that they all
tend to erase, or at least blur more and more, the line which
divides the old order from the Revolution—and, for that
matter, the Revolution from what followed in the next
century. Recent scholarly literature thus forces the mind back

to questions of definition which faced us at the outset—where does the Revolution begin? Where does it end? And these, in turn, raise the most puzzling question of all: what *was* the Revolution?

Its scale has always been easier to assess than its nature. For good or ill, it was a cataclysm, and it remains one in historical visions of it entertained by many people. This is not always very conscious; often they are hardly aware of how brusque a disruption of French history such categorizations as the triumph of a class may imply. But whether seen as bringing a new heaven and a new earth or revealing a glimpse of the pit beneath ordered society, the Revolution has always found ready acknowledgement of its transforming power. Its contemporaries, of course, felt its force in a very personal way—or, at least, millions of Europeans did; it must never be forgotten that the Revolution happened, in the end, to men and women, not to abstractions of class and occupational group.

This overwhelming impact, the most immediately recognizable characteristic of the Revolution, has prompted many attempts to pin down its nature in a general statement. A few only among them have been glanced at here. That we now find them inadequate should not disguise from us the intellectual as well as emotional satisfaction they once gave; there is an inherent and overall plausibility to such formulations which must be given due weight. They did not merely express easily touched-off fears and hopes; they reflected the experience of thousands of people and the indirect impact of events on millions who had their lives changed utterly by the processes which burst through the surface first in 1789 and the events which followed. Equally, the vast scope of the theoretical and institutional innovations made possible by the Revolution supports the view that it was one of the great turning-points of modern history, an epoch-marking phenomenon. A vast advancement of liberty and individualism was then achieved in principle and men rightly sensed a new beginning.

The difficulty remains that so wide-ranging and so vaguely outlined are many of the changes which make up the whole process we call 'the Revolution' that it is almost impossible to sum them up in a characterizing phrase which does not distort them. It is difficult, too, to leave room in any characterization for that recognition of what did *not* change which is so inseparable a part of what happened in the 1790s. Finally, wherever the weight of definition falls, it must not obscure the fact that so much of what changed did so only *in posse*; if, for instance, we confine our gaze to the old battleground of what happened to 'classes' (to use that dangerously anachronistic term) we have to remember that the Revolution changed the relationship of occupational and economic groups to one another less than it changed the institutions through which those relationships would have to work in the future, the mentality through which they could express themselves, and the economic possibilities which would modify their operation and therefore their nature. The people who had power and wealth before the Revolution were not very unlike those who had them afterwards; what was new was the freedom they gained from it to exploit such advantages.

If we must have one word to characterize this, let it be the fashionable term 'modernization'. This may be defined as the removal of the social encumbrances presented by the circumscribing of human possibilities by status, by un-examined belief usually expressed in supernatural categories, and by the subordination of economic and technological to social and moral criteria. The French Revolution initiated the most concentrated example of such a change to be seen before the nineteenth century; all round the world similar changes have since then brought an enormous (though ambiguous) liberation from the past, opening the way to new brutalities in the place of old, to new superstitions and dogmatisms as well as to new possibilities and aspirations. Wherever it has occurred and has been pressed home, the imposition of modernity has been painful and distressing to some—often to many. England, the United States, and the Dutch republic were much more 'modern' than France even after the Revolution, but had evolved so far fairly slowly; France suddenly began to be able to move faster in 1789 in the same direction, benefiting less from organic development than they had done, but perhaps for that reason formulating more clearly than any other country much of what was implied in a change to a new view of society. This, of course, also explained much of her violence.

This justifies a summary of the acceleration of history in France which began in the late 1780s as above all a great release. The search for single or overreaching causes for the Revolution (often at the expense of appreciating its effects) has for a long time detracted historians and laymen alike from the sociological truism which lay at the root of Burke's analysis: if you loosen any joint or timber in a society, consequential shifts and adjustments will occur throughout the whole structure and increase the likelihood of further shifts. In the end, social collapse, when not engineered from without by a greater disaster, is a cumulative process. The multitude of disconnected, uncoordinated, no longer compensated strains in French society in 1789 achieved, thanks to the circumstances of that year, a sudden and huge release. For a few years, there was what even now seems an astonishing outburst throughout society of forces hitherto pent-up; an atmosphere was generated in which an anarchy of purposes, some parallel, some conflicting, could play upon one another and on a social fabric suddenly without many of the props, braces, buttresses which had determined its shape for centuries. The intensity and turbulence which followed, because of the huge possibilities to which they opened the way (and not merely in France), now seem more remarkable than conscious innovation as motors of change. We ought not to try to make them look too tidy.

There is perhaps some positive direction for the historian in such an interpretation, too. It is at least one possible conclusion that it points us towards a revaluation of the events and political history of the great decade of the 1790s. If the Revolution was, after all, a crisis in a much slower evolution, an outbreak into uncontrollability, this provided the chance of a new sort of politics. A zone appeared in which the play of circumstance, personality, and sheer fortune were for a short time at their maximum; this suggests that the exploration of the play of influence and power at the centre should again claim our attention. There is no need to return to the incense-laden atmosphere of Robespierrolatry or to the demonology of his detractors, but we need just as much to know what it was that made the shifting coalitions of the Convention (for example) work as we need to know how the *Maximum* was (or was not) enforced in a particular department.

In spite of alarmist responses from those who sense a decline in the importance of their subject and in spite of our new sense of the continuities linking past and future in the Revolution, none of this diminishes its towering importance as an episode in the history of France and the world. It is inconceivable that this could ever be lost to sight, for it underlies a continuing myth central to the politics of western civilization and, now therefore, to those of the world. What happened in France between 1789 and 1795 bequeathed to the world the vision of revolution as a universal experience, whether for good or ill, a new view of politics related to that universal idea, and the notion that at the heart of progress lay liberation from the past, secularization, egalitarianism, and rationalism. The notion that there might be for the community—even the community of the whole human race— only one valid and correct answer to its problems was immeasurably strengthened after a short period in which it seemed that in its older religious forms such an idea was on the wane. The liberal and left-wing tradition stemming from this remained conscious and acknowledged at least as late as the Bolshevik Revolution; its unconscious applications continue still. Even when it handicaps them in other ways, many men still find it easy to recognize their own politics and those of their opponents alike when they are defined in terms whose roots lie in the hopes and fears of the Great Revolution.

Further reading in English

IT is now possible to go a fair way into the history of the French Revolution without reading French. Not only have standard French books been translated, but many important original contributions have been made to the literature in recent years by scholars writing in English. As this book was from the start intended for those who might not be able to read French it seems useful to add to it a few notes based on the same principle about further reading; with one exception, only work available in English is mentioned in what follows. It hardly need be said that the result is not a comprehensive bibliography even within that limitation; it is only an attempt to provide some guidance about where to go next.

The obvious starting-point is a selection from the large number of general accounts available. The most comprehensive is a two-volume translation of a big book by Georges Lefebvre, entitled *The French Revolution: From its Origins to 1793* (1962—unless a place of publication is mentioned in these notes, it is London) and *The French Revolution: From 1793 to 1799* (1964). Though they focus on France (and have helpful bibliographies) these two volumes are world-wide in scope. Professor G. Rudé covers a narrower geographical front and a longer chronological sweep in smaller compass in his Fontana volume *Revolutionary Europe, 1783–1815* (1964). Like Lefebvre's work, this sets the French Revolution against an international background; in the setting of purely French history, the best brief introduction is still A. Cobban's *A History of Modern France. I. 1715–1799* (rev. edn. 1965).

The decade 1789–99 has been traditionally taken to include the most important events of the Revolution, however we define it. Many narratives describe it at length. Two translations are still valuable for the mass of information they contain, their classical standing, and their organization. One is *The French Revolution, a Political History, 1789–1804* (1910) by the great Alphonse Aulard, the other is by his critic A. Mathiez, *The French Revolution* (1928). From many single-volume accounts by English historians, four may be selected, of which the oldest is the learned, enjoyable, and now somewhat out-of-date book by J. M. Thompson, *The French Revolution* (Oxford, 1944). It only takes the story down to Robespierre's fall, but it is within this limitation a richly detailed and valuable (as well as highly personal) synthesis of the pre-war scholarship. A much shorter book, also called *The French Revolution*, was published in 1953 by Professor A.

Goodwin; it offers a slim account of the political unfolding of the Revolution which is arguably still the most lucid available. The next important general book in English was *A Social History of the French Revolution* by Professor Norman Hampson (1963), a beautiful synthesis of post-Thompson research which, thanks to its approach, broke with the conventional political framework of exposition. Though still not going beyond 1795, it remains the best starting-point for the student. *The French Revolution* by Professor M. J. Sydenham, which appeared in 1965, should also be noted. It compares favourably with Thompson's book written twenty years earlier and is in a measure its replacement. Like his predecessor, Professor Sydenham offers a narrative, but one shorter, less discursive, and, of course, more up-to-date. His subsequent book, *The First French Republic 1792–1804* (1974), overlaps the earlier in coverage and at last provided a fresh narrative account in English of the later years of the decade. To all these must finally be added the translation of a work by Professor Albert Soboul, *The French Revolution, 1787–1799* (1974), a book doubly interesting, since it presents an overtly Marxist interpretation of the Revolution and is written by the scholar who dominates the academic study of the Revolution in France today.

Next come a number of interpretative and general works which do not easily fit into particular topical categories, but which must be considered. The late Alfred Cobban detonated a lively controversy with the publication of his lectures on *The Social Interpretation of the French Revolution* (Cambridge, 1964). On the debate which followed, it is still worth reading Miss C. B. A. Behrens' review article 'Professor Cobban and his Critic' in *The Historical Journal*, 1966. Many other interesting pieces by Cobban have been reprinted in two volumes of his papers entitled *Aspects of the French Revolution* (1968) and *France Since the Revolution* (1970). Professor Richard Cobb's approach is a very different one from Cobban's (he was the author of a review which especially drew Miss Behrens' fire) and is rooted in long residence in France and experience of French archives. In some ways, the best introduction to his work is to be found in two pieces: 'Au car de Milly', a splendid evocation by an enthusiast of the delights of archival study in France, and 'Experiences of an Anglo-French Historian', both reprinted in a book called *A Second Identity: Essays on France & French History* (1969). But Professor Cobb's work oozes personality and autobiography and there are many other starting-points almost as enthralling. What is *not* available in English, unfortunately, is his finest book, a study of the *armées révolutionnaires* of 1793–4, which has a firmness of structure (thanks, no doubt, to the possibility of focusing on one institution's growth, change, and demise) that his others lack. They, instead, are unified by approach and temperament rather than theme; no comparable body of work (outside collections of documents themselves) displays so much of the variety, the individual, the marginal, and the forgotten sides of the Revolution. To the almost complete exclusion of a traditional political narrative, they provide a series of unique explorations of the social history of the Revolution at ground-level (and a unique illumination of its sources, too). The most important of these books are *The Police and The People: French Popular Protest 1789–1820* (Oxford, 1970), *Reactions to the French Revolution* (1972), and *Paris and its Provinces* (1975).

Few books could be more different from these than the useful collection of short statements of some interpretative theses about the Revolution edited by Dr. P. Amann, *The Eighteenth-Century Revolution: French or Western?* (Boston, 1963). Professor Rudé's useful pamphlet for the Historical Association, *Interpretations of the French Revolution* (1961), Professor J. H. Stewart's *The French Revolution: Some Trends in Historical Writing 1945–65* (Washington, D.C., 1967), and the wider-ranging chapter by Professor the Rev. John McManners, on 'The Historiography of the French Revolution' in Volume VIII of *The New Cambridge Modern History*, discuss similar topics. Finally, in any discussion of interpretation it should be noticed that there are many reprints of English translations of Tocqueville's great book. The first (by Henry Reeve) is by and large still the best, but it is probably easier to buy a recent version by Dr. Hugh Brogan entitled *The Ancien Régime and the French Revolution* (1974).

The approach to the Revolution of 1789 was the ostensible subject of Tocqueville's book, and several books which deal with aspects of it in their pursuit of other themes call for remark. On the institutional side, for example, J. Bosher's study, *French Finances 1770–1795* (Cambridge, 1970) is very helpful, and social history is clarified by two valuable books by Professor Olwen Hufton, *Bayeux in the Late Eighteenth Century* (Oxford, 1967) and *The Poor of Eighteenth-Century France 1750–1789* (Oxford, 1974). French social history is perhaps the area of research in which English-speaking historians have contributed most to our understanding of the old order. Professor Robert Forster has added importantly to our knowledge of the nobility (and to the quickening of controversy about it) in a large number of papers and books. Especial mention may be made of 'The Provincial Noble: a Reappraisal' (*American Historical Review*, 1963), his book on the history of a single family, *The House of Saulx-Tavanes* (1971), and his study of *The Nobility of Toulouse in the Eighteenth Century* (Baltimore, 1960). Another American scholar, Professor G. V. Taylor, has helped to explain the role of noblemen in business before the Revolution in two articles on 'Types of Capitalism in Eighteenth-Century France' (*English Historical Review*, 1964) and 'Noncapitalist Wealth and the Origins of the French Revolution' (*American Historical Review*, 1967).

The *parlementaires* were very important within the nobility and *The Parlement of Bordeaux at the End of the Old Regime 1771–1790* by Dr. W. Doyle (1974) is an admirable help in understanding them. For the light it throws on local and religious history, too, this book may usefully be coupled here with a study of a later period, Dr. Alan Forrest's *Society and Politics in Revolutionary Bordeaux* (Oxford, 1975). Dr. Doyle has also written two important and controversial articles on different aspects of the general story of the nobility under the old order, 'The Parlements of France and the Breakdown of the Old Régime' (*French Historical Studies*, 1970) and 'Was there an Aristocratic Reaction in Pre-Revolutionary France?' (*Past and*

Present, 1972). In the latter journal also appeared 'Nobles, Bourgeois and the Origins of the French Revolution' (1973), an article of importance and insight by Dr. Colin Lucas: together with Dr. Doyle's article and some other essays from *Past and Present*, it has since been reprinted in *French Society and the Revolution* (Cambridge, 1976) edited by Professor Douglas Johnson. Such writings as these lead naturally to a consideration of the political 'Pre-Revolution', but it has not received much specialized attention in English since an important paper by Professor Goodwin, 'Calonne, the Assembly of French Notables of 1787 and the Origins of the "Révolte Nobiliaire"' (*English Historical Review*, 1946). The translation of an important synthesis by Georges Lefebvre, *The coming of the French Revolution* (Princeton, 1947) goes some way towards filling this gap (and incidentally provides the surprising information that Louis' queen 'declared herself ravished on receiving a deputation from the National Guard'). On the question of peasant discontent, to our understanding of which Lefebvre contributed so much, an article by Professor Alun Davies, 'The Origins of the French Peasant Revolution of 1789' (*History*, 1964) is still helpful. Another valuable translation covering much of the first year of the Revolution is *The Taking of the Bastille July 14th, 1789* by Jacques Godechot (1970). Apart from these, the English reader must fall back upon Cobban's narrative account for the pre-Revolutionary crisis.

Before plunging into monographs which illuminate different aspects of the Revolution during the 1790s, it is useful to consider such biographies as are available to the English reader. J. M. Thompson's collection of sketches of *Leaders of the French Revolution* (Oxford, 1929) can still be read with profit and pleasure and his major book (other than this general history) was a biography, *Robespierre* (Oxford, one-volume edn. 1939), the best synthesis in any language of the results of Mathiez's long exploration of the details of his hero's career. What Thompson's book lacks is the perspective upon the great Incorruptible made available by later research directed more especially to the social setting of Parisian politics and the working of government during the Terror. This has been distilled and taken into account in a book by Norman Hampson, *The Life and Opinions of Maximilien Robespierre* (1974) which is rather a debate on Robespierre and what he stood for than a biography; together with Thompson's, though, it will satisfy most enquirers. Mention may also be made of a good choice of documents in translation focused on the last phase of Robespierre's life, *The Ninth Thermidor*, by the American scholar, Dr. R. T. Bienvenu (New York, 1968). Among other biographies in English, Leo Gershoy's *Barère, A Reluctant Terrorist* (Princeton, 1962) is very illuminating, and although Louis Gottschalk's *Jean Paul Marat: a study in radicalism* is old, many students still find it a stimulating book. It has been reprinted as a paperback (Chicago, 1967). Gottschalk has also published five volumes of a biography of Lafayette which are somewhat heavy going, but the last two contain much useful information about the early Revolution. They were written in co-operation with Dr. M. Maddox and are entitled *Lafayette in the French Revolution, through the October Days* and *Lafayette in the French Revolution, from the October days through the Federation* (Chicago, 1969 and 1973). Apart from these, there is a shortage of scholarly biographical studies of the great revolutionaries. One of the Directors though, is the subject of an old book by J. H. Clapham, *The Abbé Sieyès* (1912), which is still worth reading. *Mirabeau* by O. J. G. Welch (1951) is also useful, as is E. N. Curtis' book, *Saint Just, Colleague of Robespierre* (New York, 1935). But that is about all that we have available in English.

Within the Revolutionary decade, many important contributions have been made to our knowledge of special themes by writers in English. A brilliant condensation of religious history can be found in Professor J. McManners' little book on *The French Revolution and the Church* (1969). Two specialized and important articles by Mr. M. Hutt are 'The Role of the Curés in the Estates General' and 'The Curés and the Third Estate' (*Journal of Ecclesiastical History*, 1955, 1957). *French Protestantism and the French Revolution*, a study by B. C. Poland (Princeton, 1957) is helpful, and an interesting article by James N. Hood explores 'Protestant–Catholic Relations and the Roots of the First Popular Counterrevolutionary Movement in France' (*Journal of Modern History*, 1971).

So far as Paris is concerned, the books of Professor George Rudé have been very influential. Two will be found good starting-points, *The Crowd in the French Revolution* (Oxford, 1959) and *Paris and London in the 18th Century: Studies in Popular Protest* (1970), a collection of reprinted pieces. Part of Soboul's thesis on the *sansculottes* has been translated with the title *The Parisian Sans-Culottes and the French Revolution 1793–4* (Oxford, 1964), but it omits much of the most interesting material in that study. On the provinces, there are several important studies in English. To those by Professor Hufton and Dr. Forrest which have already been noticed may be added Dr. W. Scott's book on *Terror and Repression in Revolutionary Marseilles* (1973), an article by T. J. A. Le Goff and D. M. G. Sutherland on 'The Revolution and The Rural Community in Eighteenth-Century Brittany' (*Past and Present*, 1974), and another by R. B. Rose on 'Tax Revolt and Popular Organisation in Picardy 1789–1791' (Ibid., 1969). Dr. Colin Lucas has shown how Revolutionary institutions worked in a particular locality in his book on *The Structure of the Terror: the example of Javogues and the Loire* (Oxford, 1973), and such local studies (as he shows) blur easily into the history of the Counter-Revolution; this is manifest in the study of *The Vendée* by Professor C. Tilly (1964). Foreign connections with counter-revolution have been explored with the aid of British records by Dr. Harvey Mitchell in his study of *The Underground War against Revolutionary France: the Missions of William Wickham 1794–1800* (Oxford, 1965), and by Professor W. R. Fryer in *Republic or Restoration in France, 1794–7* (Manchester, 1965).

Such books return the reader to the political history of the Revolution. The years of the Constituent and Legislative are less well-represented by up-to-date work in English than later periods, but the old study of *Barnave* (Oxford, 1915) by E. D. Bradby is still not valueless. For the period of what is called the 'great' Committee of Public Safety—when it was dominated by Robespierre—there is much help to be obtained from the best book by a veteran American scholar, Professor R. R. Palmer's *Twelve Who Ruled* (Princeton, 1941). Old misconceptions and myths about *The Girondins* were (one hopes) finally disposed of in a book with this title by M. J. Sydenham (1961), and a gallant (and highly complex) attack on the problems of the internal politics of the Convention by means of data on voting has been made by Dr. Alison Patrick's *The Men of the First French Republic* (Baltimore, 1973). A book by Dr. Isser Woloch, with the title *Jacobin Legacy* (Princeton, 1970), carries the political story forward into the period of the Directory.

The Directory now shows signs of being one of the most interesting zones due for exploration in the next few years. An important step was taken by an English historian forty years ago, when Professor Goodwin published an article in the periodical *History* in 1937 entitled 'The French Executive Directory: a revaluation'. In a small compass it raised many important questions which for the most part remained ignored until the 1960s. Then Dr. C. H. Church wrote a thesis on problems of central government under the Directory and followed this with a general discussion in an essay published in a memorial volume for Cobban (*French Government and Society*, 1973) entitled 'In Search of the Directory' (two other essays by him on the bureaucracy of the Revolutionary era may usefully be consulted in *Past and Present*, 1967, and *French Historical Studies*, 1970). Since then, Dr. Martin Lyons has published a book, *France under the Directory* (1975) and the latest contribution to the illumination of the regime is provided in an article by Dr. Lucas on 'The First Directory and the Rule of Law' in *French Historical Studies*, 1977.

One or two useful books tend to escape even so loosely organized a grouping as that of this introductory essay. Dr. D. Greer's statistical studies of *The Incidence of the Terror during the French Revolution* (Cambridge, Mass., 1935) and of *The Incidence of the Emigration during the French Revolution* (Cambridge, Mass., 1951) are among these; another is S. G. Harris, *The Assignats* (Cambridge, Mass., 1930).

Table of events and dates before 1800

1787	February 22:	Meeting of first (Calonne's) Assembly of Notables
1788	August 8:	Decision to assemble the Estates-General
	25:	Necker enters royal ministry
	September 25:	The Paris *Parlement* recommends the Estates-General be held as in 1614
	November 6:	Meeting of second Assembly of Notables
	December 27:	Decision of royal council on numbers of the Third Estate (the *doublement*)
1789	May 5:	Estates-General assemble at Versailles
	June 17:	Adoption of title 'National Assembly' by the Third Estate
	19:	Majority of clergy vote to join the Third Estate
	20:	Excluded from their meeting-place, the members of the Third Estate assemble in a tennis court and swear not to disband until a constitution is established
	23:	The royal session (*séance royale*)
	27:	The clergy and nobility are ordered by the King to join the Third Estate
	July 11:	Necker dismissed
	14:	The fall of the Bastille
	16:	Recall of Necker
	20:	The beginning of the worst phase of the 'Great Fear'
	August 5–11:	Decrees of the National Assembly abolishing 'feudalism' and much of the historic structure of French society
	26:	National Assembly approves the text of a Declaration of the Rights of Man and the Citizen
	September 11:	Vote on the proposal to give a suspensive veto on legislation to the King
	October 5–6:	The 'October Days' followed by removal of the royal family and National Assembly to Paris

	10:	Louis XVI decreed 'King of the French'
	21:	Decree on public order (*loi martiale*)
	29:	Decree distinguishing electoral rights of 'active' and 'passive' citizens
	November 2:	Assumption by the State of the property of the Church
	7:	Decree closing ministerial posts to deputies of the Constituent
	December 14–22:	Legislation reorganizing local government
	19:	First issue of *assignats*
1790	January 28:	Removal of civic disabilities of Jews
	February 13:	Suppression of religious orders (unless engaged in teaching or charitable work) and of monastic vows
	March 15:	Decree on terms of redemption of seigneurial dues
	May 22:	Renunciation of wars of conquest by the Constituent
	June 11:	Inhabitants of Avignon declare their wish to form part of France
	19:	Decree abolishing titles and status of hereditary nobility
	July 12:	The Civil Constitution of the Clergy
	14:	First public celebration of Bastille day (*fête de la fédération*)
	September 4:	Necker resigns from ministry
	October 26:	First authorization by the King of overtures to foreign courts on possible intervention by them in France
	29:	Black rebellion in San Domingo
	November 27:	First decree imposing civic oath on clergy
1791	February 9:	First bishops of constitutional church elected
	March 2:	Abolition of guilds and monopolies
	10:	Pope's pastoral letter condemning Civil Constitution and Declaration of Rights of Man
	April 13:	Papal Bull *Caritas* condemns the Civil Constitution
	May 15:	Black inhabitants of French colonies who are born of free parents are declared equal in civic rights with whites
	June 14:	Combination Law (*Loi le Chapelier*)
	20:	The King leaves Paris for the abortive 'flight to Varennes'
	25:	The King suspended from his functions on returning, under duress, to Paris
	July 15:	The King declared inviolable by the Assembly and he is restored to his prerogatives

17:	Firing on crowd by National Guardsmen when disturbances occur at the signing of a petition against the King's reinstatement (the 'massacre of the *Champ de Mars*')
August 17:	All Frenchmen abroad are summoned to return within one month
27:	The Declaration of Pillnitz by the king of Prussia and emperor of Austria
September 14:	The King formally accepts the Constitution and is restored to his functions. Avignon annexed
28:	Abolition of slavery in France, but not in the colonies
30:	The Constituent Assembly dissolves
October 1:	First meeting of the Legislative Assembly
November 9:	Decree declaring emigrants suspect of conspiracy against the nation orders their return
12:	Royal veto of decree of 9 November against emigrants
29:	Decree against non-juring priests
December 19:	Royal veto of decree of 29 November against non-juring priests
1792 January 2:	Decree that 1 January 1789 shall be reckoned the start of the 'era of liberty'
February 9:	Property of emigrants declared forfeit to the nation
March 10–23:	Ministry forced to resign by Legislative and a 'Brissotin' ministry is appointed in its stead
April 5–6:	Decree suppressing Sorbonne and all religious congregations
20:	Declaration of War on the 'King of Hungary and Bohemia' (Austria, in effect)
June 12:	King dismisses 'Brissotins' and appoints a more royalist ministry
19:	Royal veto of another decree against non-juring priests and of a decree providing for the assembly of a military camp at Paris
20:	A mob invades the royal palace of the Tuileries, where the King and royal family are insulted and menaced
July 11:	Decree authorizing the country to be proclaimed to be 'in danger'
21:	The country proclaimed 'in danger'
25:	Manifesto by the duke of Brunswick threatens Paris with dire consequences if the city does not submit to the King

25:	The Assemblies of the Paris 'Sections' are authorized to sit continuously (*en permanence*)
28:	News of the Brunswick Manifesto reaches Paris
31:	The Paris section Mauconseil invites other sections to join it in a demonstration in the Assembly demanding the deposing of the King
August 3:	Petition from 47 out of 48 Paris sections demands deposing of the King
9:	The Assembly sets aside consideration of republican petitions, and a 'revolutionary commune' usurps the government of Paris
10:	Insurrection: the storming of the Tuileries is followed by the suspension of the King from his functions and the reinstatement of ministers dismissed in June (ministry of Roland)
19:	Lafayette defects to the Austrians
23:	Prussian army takes Longwy
25:	Redemption charges for seigneurial dues abolished
September 2:	Prussian army takes Verdun
2–6:	Prisoners murdered in Paris (the 'September Massacres')
20:	Prussians defeated at Valmy
21:	First public session of the Convention, constituted the day before; the monarchy abolished by unanimous vote
22:	Convention orders that all acts are in future to be dated from the year 1 of the 'Republic', the first time the word is officially used
29:	French occupation of Nice (Sardinian territory)
October 1:	Prussians abandon Champagne
21:	French troops enter Mainz
November 6:	Battle of Jemappes; French invasion of Belgium under way
19:	Decree offering aid to subject people wishing to be free
27:	Decree making Savoy (formerly Sardinian) a French Department (the 84th)
December 15:	Decree on exploitation and government of conquered territories
1793 January 14–17:	The Convention takes its decision on the fate of the King
21:	Execution of the King
24:	The French ambassador ordered to leave the United Kingdom by the British government

February 1:	Declaration of war on the United Kingdom and the Dutch republic
14:	Principality of Monaco annexed
March 7:	Declaration of war on Spain
9:	First authorization of missions by members of the Convention (*représentants en mission*) to the provinces and armies
10:	Decree setting up the Revolutionary Tribunal
11:	Opening of rising in the Vendée
18:	Battle of Neerwinden followed by abandonment of Netherlands by French army
21:	*Comités de surveillance* set up in each commune
April 6:	First Committee of Public Safety (set up 26 March) reduced to 9 members; General Dumouriz (Fr. commander at Neerwinden) defects to Austrians
May 4:	The first *Maximum*, on grain prices
May 31–June 2:	Insurrection followed by suspension and arrest of some members of the Convention ('the fall of the Gironde') and a purge of all government committees except the Committee of Public Safety
June 6:	'Federalist' movements against the Convention at Bordeaux and Marseilles
24:	Voting of the Constitution of 1793
July 17:	Final abolition of all feudal rights without compensation
26:	Decree against hoarding (*accaparement*), which becomes a capital crime
27:	Robespierre joins the Committee of Public Safety
28:	Loss of Valenciennes
August 1:	Adoption of the metric system and order for the arrest of all nationals of countries with which the Republic is at war, unless resident in France before 14 July 1789
23:	decree of *levée en masse* (universal obligation to service)
27:	Toulon surrendered to British and Sardinians
September 5:	Parisian insurrection secures further radicalization of the war-effort by the Convention; 'terror' is henceforth the order of the day
17:	Law of Suspects
22:	Beginning of the 'Year II' of the revolutionary calendar (the calendar was inaugurated on 7 October)

	29:	New law of the general *Maximum* on prices and wages
October 9:		Reconquest of Lyons, in 'feudalist' hands since May
	10:	Decree declaring 'revolutionary government'
	16:	Execution of Marie Antoinette
	24–31:	Trial followed by execution of the 'Girondin' leaders
December 4:		Law of 14 *Frimaire* on Revolutionary Government
	19:	British leave Toulon
	23:	Last important republican victory in the Vendée, henceforth the scene only of guerrilla war
1794 January 27:		Convention decrees the appointment of teachers of the French language in regions where the inhabitants do not speak French
February 4:		Abolition of slavery in French colonies
	21:	Revision of the *Maximum*
March 14–24:		Arrest, trial, and execution of 'Hébertist' extremists
March 30–April 5:		Arrest, trial, and execution of 'Dantonists'
April 27:		New police law (of 27 *Germinal*)
May 18:		Victory of Tourcoing over British in Belgium
June 1:		The 'Glorious First of June'; British naval victory
	8:	Festival of the Supreme Being (20 *Prairial*)
	10:	Law of 22 *Prairial* speeds up work of Revolutionary Tribunal by removing safeguards protecting prisoners
	16:	Battle of Fleurus, followed by French reconquest of Belgium
July 23:		New scales of wages imposed by Commune of Paris
	26:	Robespierre's last speech in the Convention calls for a new purge
	27:	The '9th *Thermidor*'; denunciation of Robespierre and his cronies; abolition of Commune of Paris by the Convention
	28:	Execution of Robespierre; 115 others are guillotined on this and the following day
	30–31:	Reorganization of Committee of Public Safety
August 10:		Reorganization of the Revolutionary Tribunal
September 18:		Financial support by the State of all forms of religious worship withdrawn
November 12:		Closing of Jacobin Club
December 8:		Return of some 'Girondins' to Convention

	24:	Abolition of the *Maximum*
1795	February 21:	Decree providing for freedom of worship and separation of Church and State
	April 1:	*Sansculotte* insurrection of 12 *Germinal*
	5:	Peace with Prussia signed at Basle
	May 16:	Peace with United Provinces signed and recognition by France of the 'Batavian Republic'
	20:	Insurrection of 1 *Prairial* by sansculottes
	23:	Disarmament of Paris sections by the army
	May–June	'White Terror' in the South; many murders of former terrorists by royalists
	June 8:	Death of Louis XVII in captivity: the comte de Provence becomes Louis XVIII
	July 22:	Peace with Spain signed
	August 22:	Convention approves the 'Constitution of the Year III'
	October 5:	Defeat of attempted Parisian insurrection of 13 *Vendémiaire*
	26:	Convention disperses; the Directory is inaugurated and the *Place de la Révolution* is renamed *Place de la Concorde*
1796	April 28:	Armistice of Cherasco with Sardinia
1797	May 12:	Democratic republic set up at Venice
	June 15:	Ligurian republic set up at Genoa
	July 9:	Cisalpine republic set up at Milan
	September 4:	*Coup d'état* of 18 *Fructidor*; legislature purged
	October 17:	Peace with Austria (Treaty of Campo Formio)
1798	February 15:	Proclamation of Roman republic
	April 12:	Proclamation of Helvetic republic
	May 11:	*Coup d'état* of 22 *Floréal*; legislature purged
	August 1:	French fleet destroyed in Battle of the Nile
1799	January 26:	Proclamation of satellite republic (the 'Parthenopean') at Naples
	March 12:	France declares war on Austria
	April 29:	Russians enter Milan; during the summer a succession of Russian and Austrian victories eliminates French power in Italy except for a besieged garrison at Genoa
	September 25–7:	Russians defeated at Zurich and subsequently leave Switzerland
	November 9–10:	Bonaparte's *coup d'état* of 18–19 *Brumaire*

Index